M000221933

God, I Forgive You

God, I Forgive You

by Shanda Miller

Copyright 2020 Shanda Miller

Total Fusion Press
PO Box 123
Strasburg, OH 44680
www.totalfusionpress.com

All rights reserved. No part of this book may be reproduced or transmitted in any form or by any means, electronic or mechanical, including photocopying and recording, or by any information storage or retrieval system, without permission in writing from the publisher or author.

While this book is a true account and based on facts, memories, and personal family documents and photos, the conversations recounted are not word-for-word. The stories have been recreated from memories to give the reader a better sense of the individuals involved. The names of some individuals have been changed to protect their identities.

ISBN (paperback): 978-1-943496-14-3

Editor: Kara D. Starcher
Front cover design: Josh Aul, Nexlevel Design, LLC, www.nexleveldesign.com

Unless otherwise noted, all Scripture quotations are taken from the New King James Version®. Copyright © 1982 by Thomas Nelson. Used by permission. All rights reserved.

Scripture quotations marked (NLT) are taken from the Holy Bible, New Living Translation, copyright ©1996, 2004, 2015 by Tyndale House Foundation. Used by permission of Tyndale House Publishers, a Division of Tyndale House Ministries, Carol Stream, Illinois 60188. All rights reserved.

Published in Association with Total Fusion Ministries, Strasburg, OH
www.totalfusionministries.org

29 28 27 26 25 24 23 22 21 20   1 2 3 4 5

To Tommy,
For always being my safe place.
I would follow you to the ends of the earth.
No matter what, house or hut.

Contents

Foreword

Can you forgive God?

"No one had to tell me to 'be quiet, lay flat, or keep a secret.' Those things were life and death in my family."—Shanda Miller.

Growing up in a life of murder, violence, pain, and abuse from your own family, and knowing the God of the Bible exists, leads to a conclusion: God—who is supposed to be Love, supposed to be a Savior, supposed to be all powerful and all knowing, who could step in and stop the pain at any time—did not. Is not. And if He is all these amazing things, He is certainly not for you. Not when you were five, not when you were twelve, not at that time at school, and not in your first and second marriage. Not ever. Yet He exists. Silent, distant, cold, detached—cruel.

Can you forgive this God? The very concept may seem offensive, even blasphemous—to forgive a perfect, holy being, full of light with no shadow of turning! Not only can you forgive God, you must.

As I understand it, the first part forgiveness is forgoing the right to carry a charge against someone, and thus its correlating punishment. No matter the crime, no matter if you have discerned the situation correctly or not, no matter if you are a victim or co-perpetrator. This is an act of your will.

The second is blessing the forgiven party. Desiring their success and that all their sins will be hidden. This is when forgiveness has hit your emotions.

In short, forgiveness is a miracle.

So, what do you do when the source of this miracle is the same person who you have the charges against—a lifetime of charges? To forgo the right to justice, anger, revenge. What do you do if this person is God?

That is the story of this book. It is Shanda's story, and it is her miracle. The miracle to truly trust Him with all your heart. To declare the goodness of God as the only one who never forsook you or abandoned you. To truly fail, fall down, and get up again. To redeem the time and generations. To truly overcome.

May this story affect you as it has affected me. To heal your heart, restore your hope, and reveal your true identity—the perfect, beloved child of God.

Chris Blackeby
As He Is Ministries • www.asheisministries.org

Brace yourself, you're about to embark on a literary journey that will hurt you. Then haunt you. Then heal you. What this book did for me was ravaged my excuses, stripped my justification, and eliminated my apprehensions. I was left with an overwhelming realization that God is good, God is able, and God is willing.

I have the honor of being Shanda Miller's husband of thirteen years at the time of the release of this book. I've watched the healing hand of God reach down and truly transform this young woman's life from the inside out.

For those of you that have been hurt, rejected, beaten, and forsaken, you're about to see that no broken heart is un-mendable. For those of you that have been the diabolical culprit of your own demise, you're about to see that a God of reckless and prodigal love wants to take the life that you thought you'd never be forgiven of and make it a spectacle and masterpiece to display his goodness.

I've watched as she's cried herself to sleep. I've seen her scream at the heavens and ask, "Why, God? Why did you choose me to live this life?!" and I've had the blessing of being close to her when God healed her and answered her with a soft and firm, "Nothing you've been through will be wasted." As the old adage goes, "You're only as holy as you are at home." I can verify that the healing you see taking place in the pages of this book took place in real life. His healing saved our kids, His goodness saved our marriage, and His love saved her life. I'm confident that I would not have a wife to tell you about today had it not been for God and His endless love for this beautiful woman.

As the title so boldly proclaims, I believe as you navigate the pages of this book you'll also see that all good things come down from the Father of Lights and we will rightly attribute His goodness to Him, and see that His love was calling out to you the entire time you were lost and forsaken. Come home—He's been waiting.

Tommy Miller, Husband of the Author
Founder and Pastor, Legacy Church, New Philadelphia, Ohio.

1

A Child's Cry

Dear Jesus,

Today, I pray my daddy will go to prison. My mom told me to ask you so we could be safe. No one at school knows about my life here, but if they would ask, I might tell. I think I wanna tell. I know I'm only seven, but Grammy told me you care about everything I do. She keeps me safe, and I love going to her house. It's quiet there. I'll repeat what my mom told me to pray now. Jesus, forgive us of our sin. Keep us covered with your precious blood and protect us from the enemy. Let us sleep good tonight and wake up feeling good in the morning. Watch over Mommy, Daddy, me, Jennifer, and Melissa. In Jesus' name I pray, Amen.

I remember praying that prayer to Jesus one hot summer evening in our brown shingled house in Ohio. The strangest thing about that prayer is I don't remember being afraid of my daddy or the circumstances. I can only assume that numbness hung its hat on the rung of my heart to welcome itself home. But what did I know? I was only seven.

As children grow, they trust the people and events around

them until they are given a reason not to trust. While children's minds are developing, every memory is stored. When a moment happens, the brain scans for memories to compare it to. If a frightening memory is found, a part of the brain lights up as a reminder that the old memory can happen again and leaves the person with a decision to make. Do they trust, or do they fear?

I recently took my six-month-old granddaughter to a petting zoo, and I realized that fear is taught. We rode in a horse-drawn wagon, and we could feed, pet, and touch all the animals that walked up to the wagon. I watched my granddaughter intently while a Brahma bull strolled up eager to eat. She didn't even blink. She could have cared less that the odoriferous creature had flies everywhere, had zero manners at all, and would not ask politely for a bite of the grainy pellets. She had no idea how large he was in size or that his one bite could pulverize us. Despite his smell and size, my granddaughter smiled. She reached for him with eager arms and wanted so badly to touch him. She had no fear. She hadn't yet experienced the uneasiness of fear's lurking presence.

My granddaughter had no reason to fear that massive Brahma bull because she had no memory to compare that event to. Similarly, when I prayed my prayer that night, I didn't know fear as "fear." I had been immersed in fear for seven years so perhaps my familiarity with fear made it a normal feeling. I've heard of children being born with incurable, painful diseases that would make a grown man cry, yet those children know nothing else and don't react to the severity of their condition. Perhaps they develop an immunity to the pain. Perhaps I did too. I'd even go so far as dancing with the idea that I was afraid to be afraid.

I had been taught a lot of things in my seven short years but being afraid in situations didn't feel logical. How would being afraid help me? It never helped her. It never stopped him, anyways. No matter how much my mother begged in fear, he kept her shackled with terror. It was a sick satisfaction in his eye. Even a small child, such as I, could see that.

❀

My mom worked inside the home, and my dad was a hard-working coal miner. He kept the garden, and my mom cooked and cleaned all the time. She did the best she could with three young children; however, one day, Grandfather Gerald, my father's dad, literally did a white glove test on our house. After my grandfather's graceless act of ignorance, my poor mother stayed up all night

My parents

cleaning and became obsessed with making sure everything was spotless. I will never forget what Grandfather Gerald did because my mom ripped her wrist open on a paneling nail while scrubbing the walls. Her scar became just another reminder to us all of how the man should control his home.

I knew I had to be on my best behavior at all times at home. My father had zero tolerance for any sort of mess. The pressure of how a home should be kept trickled down into my father from his father before him. After the white glove test, he now had a standard to keep Grandfather Gerald at bay. This left no time for my mom to play with us, and we definitely were not allowed to leave toys on the floor.

I remember sitting on my mom's bed one day while she was once again cleaning her room. She turned quickly and scolded me: "Get off of the bed, Shanda! You know I can't have any wrinkles."

The carpet had to be freshly swept every day. It didn't matter if it was still clean from the day before; it had to look clean so my father wouldn't accuse my mother of being a worthless, lazy excuse of a woman. She tried so hard to leave the stripes from the vacuum on the carpet, but this was not an easy task when little feet constantly trod across the carpet. There were times, to prevent her from getting beaten up by my father, that she sent me into the basement to play.

As I would walk down the old stairs leading to the basement, my mother would quickly shut the door behind me, and I would hear the sound of a short click. I was locked in the basement. A very dim light came from the tiny window where my father unloaded coal for the furnace. I knew what being locked in the basement meant, and I learned to console myself by imagining I was locked in a dungeon and I soon would be saved. Any other child would be frantic to know they were locked inside an old, damp basement but I explored my dungeon and found many interesting treasures. In order to pass the unknown amount of time, I investigated each box my mom had stored in the basement.

Eventually, the floors above me would creak indicating that it was now safe to knock on the door to be let out of the basement. Once my father saw the marks on the carpet, we could walk on the carpet … until the next day. I was so afraid my father would hurt my mother that I would do anything she asked of me, including being locked in the basement, if it would stop him.

My mom and I had an understanding. She could tell me her secrets, and I would never tell. I remember the day she showed me the hot pink and black bathing suit she had bought for herself. She hid it in her closet beside some of the toys she purchased at a yard sale for me and my younger sister Jennifer. We never told my father because we knew there would be a punishment rendered.

I faced each day with a choice to fear or fight. I almost always chose not to fear.

Sundays were the only time I can remember quiet for more than a few hours at a time in our house. It wasn't because we were all getting along or enjoying being by ourselves. We had to be quiet. Every Sunday, my father perched himself on his throne in the living room, spellbound by the Sunday paper and football game on the television. He hated any noise that interfered with his hearing the game, and he refused to acknowledge any human life existed including my mother's who spent the time slaving away in the kitchen making a huge Sunday dinner.

Why, though? Why did they pretend? Is this what they were taught normal families did? We weren't normal and a so-called "Sunday dinner" wouldn't cut it. I never saw the point of sitting at a dinner table with people who didn't like each other and pretending everything was okay.

Needless to say, I hate the sound of football on the television. I imagine hearing the commentators chanting play after play is every sports fan's dream, but I hate it. I had every reason to hate it.

My mother eight months pregnant with Kala in April 1982

Before my youngest sister, Melissa, was born, my mother was pregnant with another little girl. (She had no idea about the sex of the baby during her entire pregnancy.) One Sunday afternoon, when she was four months pregnant, my father missed a football play because she "turned the page of the newspaper too loudly." He proceeded to beat her for disturbing his quiet. She started to experience difficulties with the pregnancy after that and could feel a popping feeling in her stomach near her navel. She told the doctor what happened and begged for another ultrasound. She had only had one ultrasound before my father hit her. Every time she asked, the doctor told her that he wouldn't do another because all she wanted was to know the sex of the baby.

My mother delivered Kala Sue, a beautiful little girl; however, my baby sister only lived for three days and passed away in my mother's arms. (She was born with Streptococcus.) I never saw her, but I was told she looked exactly like my sister Jennifer.

Both my mother and father were devastated after Kala's death.

My mother didn't want an autopsy because she couldn't bear the thought that someone would be "cutting" on her precious baby, as she called it. She also couldn't live with the thought that my father may have caused her baby girl's death. The doctor could only apologize and assume the cause of death was the separation of the umbilical cord of mother and child. There was no real evidence to determine what caused Kala's illness and death.

However, my five-year-old brain immediately blamed my father. The thought of my mother coming home without her baby almost destroyed me. As I grew older, I realized that there was no evidence to blame Kala's death on my father. I don't remember a lot being said about Kala after her funeral.

My mother swore she was done having children after Kala, but time passed, and she and my father had a little surprise. My mother gave birth to Melissa, my youngest sister. However, Melissa nearly died because she was born with spinal meningitis. After the loss of Kala, my mother was terrified seeing Melissa hooked up to so many wires as she lay in an incubator for sixteen harrowing days. Then came the most exciting news. I would get to see my baby sister. She was going to survive. That news was euphonious to my ears.

Mom, to this day, calls Melissa the miracle baby. She truly was. My mother would have been destroyed if she had to bury another child. Melissa was her "elephant print." When a person experiences a tragedy in life, that tragedy can be viewed as a bear print, a mark in their life. When a bad memory, the bear print, is replaced with a good memory, the bear print is overtaken by the elephant print, therefore aiding that person in the healing process. My mother and father were certainly in need of quite a few elephant prints.

Even though you will learn that my home life was bound in turmoil, I remember having an amazing childhood with my sister Jennifer who was two years younger. We had a yard, chickens, kittens, dogs, and rabbits, plus a tree to climb and a garden to play in. We occasionally played house and Barbie dolls, but we preferred to play outside. We loved to get up early and run out to the old chicken coop where we played house and turned mud into elegant cuisines. I would mix mud and sticks to make Jennifer omelets fit for a queen. We didn't exactly play like most girls in your run-of-the-mill activities, but we would have had it no other way.

Jennifer was my best friend, and I wanted nothing more than to protect her from the very world we lived in. She too was very protective of me. She was picked on quite a bit as a child. I saw it and the damage it did to her. Yet Jennifer was strong, unlike me. I always respected her for her strength, and she never knew how much I envied that strength while we were growing up.

I looked and acted like my mom, and Jennifer was daddy's little girl and loved him dearly. I loved him too, but part of me hated him because he liked to punish our mother a lot. It's hard to love someone when you are trying to pull him off the woman you call Mommy. I was certain my love/hate for my father was just another typical feeling.

My safe haven, until the day she died, was my grandmother, Elaine Kelley, or Grammy as I call her. I didn't know my Grammy's history when I was younger, but to know now and look back, she was not only my rock but a rock to many. She wanted to break the curse of abuse that befriended my ancestors years ago. Whether it was alcohol, physical, mental, or sexual abuse, my grandmother

Left: Me (right) riding my purple bicycle in our driveway with my sister Jennifer; Right My Grammy at age 38 holding me in 1978

was too familiar with them all. She knew what it was like to be poor, hungry, and raise babies that her own mother had abandoned and neglected. She knew what it was like to be beaten by her spouse (my biological maternal grandfather) so badly that how she survived at all should prove to an atheist that God exists. She raised her own children and endured her fair share with a few extra helpings of abuse on a level most will never understand. She is a survivor of more than many lifetimes of pain.

Life does a strange thing to people when it is unkind. Not Grammy, though. She is what I like to call an "Untouchable." She had been tested and tried throughout her life, but when she was sifted, that's when her knees were about to buckle. What do I mean by "sifted"? Sifting a person is more than just a test in life. Luke 22:31–32 says, "And the Lord said, 'Simon, Simon! Indeed, Satan has asked for you, that he may sift you as wheat. But I have prayed for you, that your faith should not fail; and when you have returned to Me, strengthen your brethren.'" Sifted in the Greek is siniazo which means "by inward agitation to shake one's faith to the point of overthrow." Simon was sifted, but the Lord prayed. He also prayed for my Grammy because he had other plans for her, and he kept her strong. She, although sifted, didn't do what they did to her. She loved them when they hated her. She gave when they took. She tried when they gave up. She held on when they let go. She prayed for them when they beat her down. Sound like anyone else you know? Maybe a lot like Jesus? She was my Grammy. The strongest woman I ever knew. She knew who Jesus was and was going to make sure her grandchildren knew him, too.

Grammy took Jennifer and me to a church several towns away from my home, and let us stay with her and Grandpa Bill often. Grandpa Bill was so fun and always made us laugh. Until the day he died, the harshest word I ever heard him say was "hammerhead." My family still giggles about that. He was not biologically related to me, and he was not anything like my other maternal grandfather, Grammy's first husband and my mother's biological father. Grandpa Bill was wise and soft-spoken, while Grandfather Alastor was tyrannical. There was no room for mistakes in his home and absolutely no occupancy available for mercy.

Grammy told me about the first time she met Jesus. Her oldest son had asked her to come to church with him. At first, she refused, but she finally gave in to his pleading. When she entered the church, she knew Jesus was there and decided to forever walk with him that day. The church was full of vibrant people; however, many were severely bound by strict religion. The rules said you should never cut your hair, and women should not wear jeans because they were men's apparel. The church taught that if you believed Jesus was in your heart, you'd go to heaven. However, you are accepted into heaven and that particular church only as long as you got in the big tub of water, spoke in strange languages, and fell on the floor a lot.

Grammy and Grandpa Bill

The church thrived on "feeling God" versus trusting God was there. So, if you didn't feel God that Sunday in the service, it meant something was wrong. Or in other words, something was wrong with you. When Grammy started taking us to church, I knew about only two books in the Bible—Revelation and Acts. Acts 2:38 to be exact. Acts told you how to be saved, and Revelation scared the literal hell right out of you. It's a scary world out there when all you're waiting for is the end of time and you're taught death is a savior.

I'm not poking fun here, please know that. I truly thought those things I mentioned in the previous paragraphs were the credentials I needed to get into those pearly gates we sang about all the time. Remember, I was young, and I thought there were three worlds—heaven where I wanted to go; hell where I thought bad people went to; and my house where I couldn't imagine hell was much worse.

My sister Jennifer and I loved Grammy's house overflowing

with warmth and happiness. Grammy's place was different too because there was no noise. It's odd to want quiet as a small child because, after all, children love colors, noise, and excitement, but I wanted peace. We could play for hours and never get bored at Grammy's. She had a small farm, and I loved all the animals. Grammy let us have mud fights and feed the baby cow along with her lambs Heckle and Jeckle. We would dig for sassafras roots in the woods down the lane and simmer them until the aroma of heaven's garden filled the house. The culminating taste of sassafras tea on a summer night at Grammy's house was my idea of peace and perfection.

At Grammy's house, I felt freedom standing at the edge of her yard. An old rickety fence was the only thing separating me from miles of farmland. I would stare into the distance watching all the beautiful colors dance together. The golds and greens waved in unison as they swayed in perfect rhythm to the resonating sounds of leaves applauding their excellence. I never wanted to leave this place of peace. I knew I could run if I wanted to. I could hide, and no one would ever find me. But in the end, I knew I had to go home.

Nothing is free. I knew I could at least enjoy freedom's company every so often. I wanted nothing more than to come back to the place where there was no chaos, only God's creation whispering to me as the winds passed by: "It's going to be okay."

❀

I was six years old when I had my first encounter with God. My babysitter told me to stay in the house while she and my sisters played outside. I must have been in trouble that particular day because everyone was outside but me. Being a little jokester, I wanted to play a prank on our cute, clueless babysitter. I truly don't know what I was thinking, but I locked the back screen door and walked out the front screen door, locking it as well on the way out. For some strange reason, I thought our babysitter would laugh, but she was not impressed when she learned that I had locked all of us out of the house. To this day, I have no idea what I was thinking, but locking the doors made sense to me at that moment.

Realizing what I had done, I ran quickly to my neighbor's house, and he came over immediately. He tried to get in and couldn't. I ran to the side of the house and took my Grammy's advice. I prayed. I was desperate. I was crying, slobbering, and making promises to God that I had no idea how I was going to own up to. I begged him with the deepest sincerity to help me because I'd be harshly punished. I knew my mom and dad were coming home soon, and I was going to get it and get it good.

The neighbor man went home and came back with the tallest ladder I had ever seen. He scooped me up on his shoulder and climbed to the tippy top of the ladder so I could reach a window. I opened the window and climbed inside.

I couldn't believe God heard me! He was real! He knew how scared I was, and I was so appreciative of his saving me from a whooping that would have caused me not to sit for a week. God cared for real, just like my Grammy said. So, I talked to him a lot after that.

My life was normal according to counselors and the average

Wearing my charm necklace for the first time. My sister Jennifer (right) wanted to take a picture with me. We were never apart.

blue-collar fellas looking from the outside in at the murky windows of my troubled home. Just like any other little girl, I went to school and wanted new clothes and little pieces of jewelry. I loved the trinkets I collected. They were simple little plastic items that reminded me of my friends at school and a few fun times. I especially loved and wanted a plastic charm necklace that all the other girls had. My mom and dad got one for me, and I'll never forget that monumental moment in my little life. I looked normal, and normalcy was important. No one at school knew anything about my other life at home.

However, I had a teacher in the first grade who had quite a temper and who reminded me that I wasn't all that far from home. Her group reading time meant being pointed out in front of everyone for what you either knew or did not know. For me, it was what I didn't know because I struggled with reading and comprehension. My mind was always somewhere else, and I just couldn't focus. Plus my teacher scared me because she never smiled. I always smiled at her. I cared about what she thought of me, and I never wanted to hurt her feelings. Nevertheless, with each day and each overlooked smile, those looks of disappointment and of failure settled into every rumple and crevice of my teacher's face.

On one particular day, the teacher told us to find the plot of a story. I didn't know what the plot was. I felt my face getting hot. Doubt had already settled in. My mouth was dry, and my shirt started sticking to me from the sweat. I thought I was feeling fear, but I was actually scared.

Each classmate, one after another, took turns whispering in the teacher's ear and pointing at the book. I wanted to see what they were pointing at so badly. I didn't care if it was cheating; I wanted to know! What were they saying to her? What is a plot and what were they pointing at? I was getting so hot I thought they all knew I didn't know the answer. Maybe they were talking about me. I felt like the only dumb person in the whole classroom. Then it happened. I was the only one left. It was my turn.

I didn't whisper or point, and I wanted to. I didn't know the only answer that mattered in my whole life just then. I didn't pray either. I was much too afraid. I couldn't think of anything but the plot! What is this plot they are speaking about? And why must we find it?

My teacher leaned in when I told her I just didn't know.

"Look again," she said.

I paused and barely shook my head No. I didn't want anyone to see. I told her the truth because I thought it would set me free. I'd get to leave the table where abandoned, dumb children sat all alone.

"Read it once more."

I could hear the agitation in her voice. I knew she was disappointed. It was killing me. It was bad enough that I didn't know, but now she was so disappointed. That look on her face will never leave my mind.

She leaned in again and repeated her first question. "Where is it, Shanda?"

I stared at the page of foreign words hoping she would disappear, but she didn't. I clutched my hair with white-knuckled hands and pulled tightly. She leaned in closer after taking a look around, and I could feel her breath hotter than fire on my face. I was so motionless that I couldn't look at her. Then I felt this burning, piercing pain shooting down my scrawny, poor excuse for an arm. She had slapped my arm! I could barely keep the tears in. My teacher left yet another welt to my collection of hidden abuse.

As soon as I hung my head and quietly cried, she apologized. An apology makes it okay. "I'm sorry" was always what made life start over at my house, so it could work here, too. She lost control, but it was okay. I made sure I didn't move so that no one else would notice. I knew how to hold still. Today, I wonder if she was truly sorry or if she was worried because that particular red handprint was visible and happened to be just her size.

I still talk to my husband, Tommy, often about that day. It took time for me to understand what fear was, but, that day, I wasn't afraid. I'd mistaken fear with humiliation. Fear is feeling in danger; humiliation is lowering the dignity of a person or self. Perhaps school was the last place I thought I still had safety and dignity, but that day it too was gone. I walked away feeling ashamed that I was not only dumb according to the outcome, but also another inconvenience to another person. I don't feel it was so much the pain of her striking me, but her face of disgust that stayed with me.

A memory of disappointment is always there without your say-so. It's much like family which never really leaves you because its veins run deep and its roots run even deeper.

I wonder if my teacher had known about my life at home, would she still have hit me? It was at that moment in time that I realized there was truly no safe place except my Grammy's house.

A baseball field neighbored our yard, and I collected all the softballs I could on hot summer days. I would wait at the edge of my yard near the skunk grass for that sweet crack of the bat meeting the softball. I'd smile and run to catch that home run knowing good and well I was keeping that souvenir. I am sure the players thought I looked like an ill-mannered puppy at the supper table, but I didn't care.

You see, my dad loved baseball, and I heard him say once that he wanted a boy so he could play baseball with him. I decided to collect all the softballs so I could play ball just like the imaginary son played with him in his wishful head. I'd be even better than that dumb boy in his fantasies. I collected quite a few softballs before I asked my dad to play. I was so excited when my mom told him to throw the ball with me that I think I ran outside faster than a child chasing an ice cream truck.

I gave my dad my collection of softballs, fairly stolen, and could not wait to play.

"Stand here next to me," he said.

I was confused at his order because we weren't standing with a gap between us like I had seen the players do, but I was much too excited to question him. He knew baseball, and I trusted him.

He threw the ball as high as he could and told me to catch it. I did. I'm not sure if I was more surprised I caught it or more surprised I didn't cry from the newfound pain in my hands. I smiled even though it stung. I'd make him proud.

He threw another one and again I caught it.

He smiled at me and said, "Good job, Shanda."

I felt satisfaction in my stomach, and it forced me to grin.

Then, I watched him walk to the back door and leave me standing there. This was not how the men played when I collected the balls. They threw back and forth and laughed and all the people clapped along.

I wondered that day if it was because I was a girl. This was the first time I felt truly let down and rejected. As a grown woman now, I know my father couldn't have meant to hurt me. He never knew how much I wanted to play. After all, much like my other life at school, he didn't ask, so I didn't tell.

I do have one other memory of playing ball with my father. My mom was standing outside with my sister and me when I grabbed an ugly, yellow Wiffle ball bat. I decided I would show my father how good I was. I had practiced with my two cousins a time or two, and I loved it! Of course, we never had more than four players, but that's what a ghost man was for. (For those of you not aware of a ghost man, let me tell you, he was the best! He could hold a base and counted as an "in" when there weren't enough players.)

I was ready, and my dad took the mound. He pitched underhand, and I swung as hard as I could. I made contact and whacked that ball.

Unfortunately, a line drive to my dad's nose was not what I had in mind. There he was bleeding all over the ground. My mother yelled at him to get in the house. I'm not going to lie, I was hoping he would jump up with a big "WOW," but the only thing coming out of him was an enormous amount of blood. He ran to the house holding his face covered in blood, and I ran to the side of the house to cry. It was the same place I went to pray when I locked us out of the house. Looking back, I wonder if that was my secret hiding spot.

Oh, I felt so bad — I had made my dad bleed. After that, I don't remember ever playing ball with him again, but maybe we did. Part of me would love to ask him in hopes of reviving even one good memory, yet, I'd be afraid to hear what a letdown I was. I had blown my one chance to prove I was worth loving. The feeling I felt that day is one I will never forget — unexpected and like it wasn't real, as if it were happening to someone else. I stood there crying and waiting to wake up from the nightmare. I had put all of my heart into the swing that would change the way my father saw me forever. I got my wish, but it wasn't the way I had intended. It did change the way he looked at me. I became the girl that could never be what he wanted.

I can still hear Grammy telling my mom, "Don't let the devil in your home. Don't let the hell in your home." As a child, I didn't know what that meant really. The only thing I could think was why would anyone let the scary devil in? Back in those days, I thought "the enemy" was a red, big-horned, scary devil waiting for you to arrive in hell to stab you with his pointy fork. I didn't know the enemy could work in and through the ones you loved and trusted. I wish the preacher man would have told me a little more about how "the enemy" worked and a little less of what he looked like. Then I would have recognized his duplicitous ways because I didn't know the scary devil ruined mommies and daddies.

At seven years old, I knew life was difficult in our home, but I didn't understand how bad it was for my mom or dad. I also had no idea how much a life could be changed by the decision of one person. The big, tall preacher man said we were in charge of our decisions, so I figured I could make my own, too. What I didn't know was I was much too small and needed a much bigger God to help me through the next transition of my life.

2

Dirty Little Secrets

Dear Jesus,

It is really happening. Everything will be different. They said I might have to leave my house, and they aren't sure where we will go. I'm a little scared, but I know I can make more friends. I pray I'm strong for her. I pray that I can take care of her and my two sisters. I pray I keep better secrets for her. Secrets like the bathing suit she bought herself and the toys she bought me at the yard sale. I never told Dad. I never told Dad about a lot of things. He hurt her when he knew. Please make him stop. Please keep us covered with your precious blood and protect us from the enemy. Let us all sleep good tonight and wake up feeling good in the morning. Watch over Mommy, Daddy, me, Jennifer, and Melissa. In Jesus' name, Amen.

It's funny what real fear does to a person. In this chapter, I am truly introduced to fear and its dull apathy to human life. It certainly is no respecter of persons and is not prejudice with any age. So, let me pave the way of this rocky and beaten path that leads to some of the most incogitable moments of my life.

Recently, I asked my husband if he'd ever been truly afraid. Not the kind of trepidation that makes you run to your bed and jump under the covers before the light goes out. Not the kind of fear that causes you to shout from a jump scare watching a Friday night thriller. I'm talking about the kind of terror that causes a shaking so great that your bed is in perfect rhythm with your body.

I can't forget that odious feeling. I can't forget that night. I see it playing in my mind like a horror movie that doesn't belong to me, but yet I own it. Every single part of it belongs to me like a child to its mother. It is forever mine to own, playing in my mind in color, every day, on repeat.

According to some of the memories I heard my father tell my mother, he didn't have an easy childhood. I had heard a few stories but figured out more whenever I stayed at my paternal grandparents' home. My father's father drank himself to inebriation quite often, and my grandmother was always there to clean up the mess. One memory my grandmother shared revolved around the frustration of frequently cleaning my grandfather's urine out of the floor registers because he was too drunk to find the bathroom.

My father was raised in a world where it was normal to have alcohol for every occasion. Every birthday Jennifer and I ever had was a party to remember. For him, that is. I mostly remember fighting with the other children about who would pump the keg, a highlight at every party. I knew how to hold the cup to keep the frothy foam out. And I knew the taste of Genesee before I was six years old. I will never forget the funny way I felt after half of a small bottle.

I don't remember my dad drinking much, but when he did,

he made his mark. Unfortunately, it was usually an imprint on my mom. Maybe he did drink every day, but I only noticed when his "beer muscles" grew and he and my mom would fight. I know now some of the reasons for my father's outrage, but nevertheless, there's never a reason to hurt a woman, especially in front of her helpless babes. She often tells me in our visits that I saved her life on more than one occasion.

I lucidly remember one evening when my mother stood in front of our kitchen stove angry at my father for yelling at her about her choice of makeup. She always looked so beautiful on the nights she and my dad would go out to play bingo or go out on the town. On this particular night she had arrayed her beautiful baby blue eyes in a bright blue eye pigment. Her jet-black eyeliner was perfect, and she had paid very close attention to every eyelash as she applied bold black layers. She was perfect that evening. She looked gorgeous, and she smelled so familiar to me—soft undertones of a leafy autumn night, highlighted with a musk of pure sexiness. That was my mom. She was as sexy as those Solid Gold Dancers that I loved watching strut across the television stage.

My dad did not like her makeup, said it was overdone, and loudly expressed his opinion to all of us in the room. I can still hear the names he called her. I was young at the time and had no idea what a whore was, but I knew it had to be bad based on how he spat the word at her. My mother stood firm and sure of herself despite what was certainly coming.

I watched as my father grabbed my mother with a firm grip

and placed both of his large, overworked hands around her skull. He pressed his thumbs so tightly to her eyelids that I was certain her eyeballs would pop out. Of course, he didn't press enough to explode her eyes, as that was not his intent. He had a purpose to his madness—her makeup was coming off.

As my father rubbed furiously, my mother screamed. She continued screaming until he reached for her throat, and then her sound turned to gasps of empty breaths interspersed with short gags. He worked his way down her neck, pressing the front of her throat with his thumbs.

I watched for what seemed like hours, every detail of every second. He was not releasing his grip on her. My eyes locked with my mother's. Her blue eyes were ruined with a hatred that washed all over her face.

By this time, they were laying on the floor in front of the stove, the large form of my father hunched over my mother. Then he clenched her throat so tightly that her tongue just hung between her drooling lips. Her eyes, once perfectly made up, were now smeared, and her eyeballs kept rolling to the back of her head. She tried to focus on me as I continued looking into her eyes.

Even at six years old, I knew she was dying.

Not knowing what else to do, I climbed up on my father's back and grabbed his hair. I ripped and ripped and ripped what I could. He finally stood up releasing his hold on my mother, and I fell to the floor. My mother gagged breath back into her lungs and my father started screaming out the rest of his rage. Shouts of blaming and cursing broke into the air. I watched her shaking, weak body try to regain strength as she tried to get her senses about her.

Everything had happened so fast. She had stared into my eyes as he choked her to near death, and I was positive I was going to be the last thing she ever saw and that moment would be the last way I saw my mother alive. Then, thankfully, she started breathing normally.

My father continued to scream and blame her for his insane, out of control violence. Suddenly, as if someone flipped a light switch, he knelt down, embraced her, and apologized once again, like the many times before. "You made me do it! I'm so sorry, baby..." Oh, how common that sentence was in our house.

This was one of the times I saved my mother. Unfortunately, it would not be the last.

My mother had no reason to even be with a man like my father. She was so radiant. She had a look about her that women grew jealous over. But, in a way, her beauty only disguised the thick emotional scars she bore. She was raised in a home that was much worse than the life my father gave her, and she had the scars to prove it.

To me, her father, my biological grandfather, Alastor, was a scary man with a constant evil look in his eyes. He was one of those people that you just sense is hiding something.

Grandfather Alastor had a sick mind. He had violently raped my mother, his daughter, from age nine until her late teens. She told me the story about one summer day when she heard men talking in the basement. She could have never known that her life was about to change forever when she went to check out those voices.

Left: Grandfather Alastor holding my sister Jennifer in 1980; Right: Grand-father Alastor in his younger years

Her father and his friend held her down as she stared out of the basement door into a field where her mother stood with a neighbor. She couldn't scream because her father shoved chunks of coal in her mouth to keep her quiet. She just lay there while both men took every ounce of her innocence away. She never had a chance against the two men. Afterward, her father threatened the lives of her siblings and her mother, my Grammy, if she told anyone. (Only one sibling later admitted to seeing it happen as they had sat on the basement steps. They were too young at the time to understand exactly what was happening and too afraid to tell what they saw.)

Well into my mother's adult years, her father continued to threaten her. When she was pregnant with me, ready to deliver, he forced her to hold the garage door up. He told her that he could kill her there and make it look like an accident. There were times after she'd married and had me that he threatened to throw me over a high wall because I drank all his milk. Some believe the threats were to keep her quiet about his abuse. Others even believed I may have been his child. (Thank the Lord for DNA testing to prove that I am not.)

I never understood why or how my mother forgave her father for the hate crimes done to her. I've battled my entire life longing to forgive him so I could feel peace. Yet, somehow she forgave him, and all of the best-kept lies were buried along with his body when I was thirteen years old. (He died from black lung; the coal mine finally caught up to him.) My mom has always chosen to forgive despite her pain. She's never held a grudge in her life, and I've always respected her for that.

My mother left home as soon as she could to marry my biological father, the first man stable enough to take care of her. As my mother often says, she "jumped out of the boiler right into the frying pan." Because of her childhood, she was a calloused spirit and hated all men. However, she needed a man in her life for stability. She didn't understand what true love meant, and she couldn't be faithful to my dad. She couldn't love him enough to even try.

My dad knew she was unfaithful. He drank to cover that pain and to entomb his own childhood abuse. He always found the courage to beat her once he grew his "beer muscles." That's what made him feel like a strong man and in control. My father was not so innocent when it came to being faithful, either. My mother would make my sister and me go to doctor's appointments with him so he wouldn't be alone around the pretty nurse. I remember the nurse's long blonde hair and her being very kind. She would take my dad back to his room while he made us stay in the big oversized black chairs. I read the children's Bible with all the colorful pictures over and over. I knew why my mom made us go. She thought if my sister and I were with my dad, he couldn't get away with cheating. It never made a difference, though. We, once again, were left in the waiting room. We were always waiting on someone to move us around. We felt like children of inconvenience, but we had each other. My sister and I would never let anyone separate us. We were strong together.

For years, my mother waited, hiding money throughout the house and gathering the courage to leave my father. I knew all about it, but I never told. I wasn't angry either. Actually, part of me was so excited about leaving that it frightened me to feel that way. I was much more afraid of that feeling than I was of my father.

My mom gathered up the courage to leave my father. She took me and my sisters to a trailer we'd never been to before. A man lived there alone and said we could stay there with him. I knew my mom really liked him. They would sneak a kiss here and there, but I pretended to never see. He was kind and soft-spoken to us and so wonderful to my mom. I had never seen her smile like she did around him. He treated us so kindly. He even let me pick what I wanted off the menu at the restaurant he took us to. It's funny how we remember the little things. Choosing my own food meant so much to me. We stayed with the kind man only for a short time, but when I look back, it seemed like an eternity.

I asked my mom where we were, and she wouldn't tell me. Mom said it was to make sure daddy didn't find us. I knew what

My mother (back) holding my youngest sister Melissa, Jennifer (left front), and me (right). This photo was taken one month before my entire life was changed forever.

she meant. I knew we were hiding. I knew if he found us, we would die this time.

Since we were hiding from my father, Jennifer and I weren't allowed to play outside and naturally started to feel cooped up inside the trailer. One day we got to swing in the front yard. I was so excited to play. Freedom! It was so hot that day, and I felt the harsh, burnt grass beneath my feet as I walked to the swing carefully keeping my eyes on the road. I tried to enjoy our playtime, but it was much like enjoying a small ice cream cone in the hot scorching sun. It was short-lived with some savored moments.

Because of my natural instinct to protect my mother, I had learned to be a hunter and not the hunted. I learned not to move. I learned to listen and not speak. I learned to watch and assume I was always being watched. I had the eyes of a true watchman.

A few nights later the man with the kind eyes took my mommy on a date, and my sisters and I stayed with my aunt and uncle. I loved going to my aunt and uncle's house. It was one of my favorite places to play. We had a younger cousin there, and we played like normal children even if only for a few hours. When we started to get tired, my sister Jennifer and I put on oversized white t-shirts that belonged to my very tall uncle. Of course, the t-shirts fit us like a nightgown down to our knobby knees, but we were okay with that.

I woke up when my mother picked me up in her arms to carry me to the kind man's truck on that warm summer evening. I felt so comfortable in my mother's arms. I can still hear the crickets and bullfrogs chattering away as if they were warning us. Perhaps I can even dance with the idea that those tiny hidden creatures were saying a prayer.

In the truck, my nine-month-old sister Melissa was already fast asleep in her car seat. The truck windows were partially down, and I could smell the hints of summer mingling with my mother's perfume, an undercurrent of a white floral breeze with a woody, vanilla musk. Oh, that familiar smell was so perfect. We all sat snug as bugs in the front seat of the truck. I was ready to drift fast asleep to the sound of the humming engine when I heard her voice.

I knew that tone.

I was a hunter, and I was aware.

I opened my eyes but refused to move. I didn't want her to hide what she was about to say. She was talking to the kind man. (I never learned his real name until much later in my life. Who was I going to tell if I knew it? I was a lost little girl that had no one to tell.)

I heard my mother say to the nice man that "he" was following us and that we needed to get away. The man insisted that he could certainly reason with him and see what he wanted. My mother begged him not to pull over.

I felt the speed of the truck accelerate, and we ended up behind a big dark red brick building. It was a high school only one town away from where we had lived with my father. My mother's voice was now calm. Maybe we were safe.

As we pulled out, within a few seconds, she shrieked that he was behind us again. I knew it was my dad. I knew and she didn't have to tell me.

The kind man decided he was pulling over at a sale barn, a place where the townsfolk bought local goods and fresh meat. The kind man had had enough—I could tell it in his voice. I also knew this would probably be the last time I'd ever see him if he got out of the truck.

The truck engine shut off. Jennifer and I were wide awake while silence filled the night air. I controlled my breathing like a hunter in the wild watching its prey. I could feel my heartbeat getting faster with each breath. The kind man assured my mom that it was all okay and they would just talk.

Then he climbed out and walked behind the truck to where my father had parked his car. Suddenly the silence was shattered with the sound of an explosion followed by a trailing echo. The echo was like yelling into a bottomless pit, hearing the sound miles away over and over. Two more shots rang out, and then dead silence.

I knew the kind man was gone, but there were no cries or screams from my sister and me. I looked up at the driver's side window and saw the eyes of a madman filled with rage. I saw that rage mixed with fear and drenched in alcohol. He was determined to end his pain along with the pain we all carried.

The window, half down, was the perfect place to rest the end of

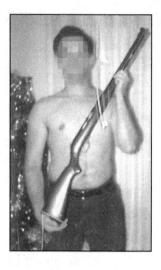

My father holding the gun
my mother had bought
for him for Christmas
only seven months earlier

the shotgun. I could see the holes where the barrel had just evicted three of its tenants to do his evil bidding. He told my mother what he was going to do. He had this planned and strategically sought out his revenge from a broken heart.

"He's dead," he said. "I'm going to kill you next and then myself. They will find us in a pile together."

However, my mother's rebuttal was not spoken to my dad. She spoke to God.

"God, if you've never heard our prayers, hear them now!"

I knew she meant it. I felt it in my spirit. She tried shoving me onto the floor, but I fought her tooth and nail so she would not be the victim of the fourth bullet.

God heard her prayer. He really heard her.

The gun jammed.

My father became confused, and my mother saw this as an opportune time to run. She opened her door and fell out of the truck. I ran after her while my sister Jennifer grabbed the car seat with our nine-month-old baby sister tucked inside. Jennifer, who was only four years old and about to turn five later that month in June, had adult strength to scoop up Melissa and her seat and run to a nearby house. Not me, though. Oh no. I wasn't leaving my mother alone with a madman. I could barely leave her alone with my father, let alone this man. It wasn't my daddy in that flesh suit that looked just like him. A crazed, abused lunatic was seizing revenge on the wrong person that night.

I watched my mother fall and trip over her feet as he chased her like a proud cat terrorizing a defeated mouse. She begged him in fear. I heard the lies coming out of her mouth one after another.

"I love you, baby," she pleaded, but he had no ears for mercy. He only had pain and anger in his eyes. It seemed as though he guarded his mind carefully, forbidding any forgiveness and mercy to come in.

A madman thinks he is a god and will take a life no matter the circumstance. It didn't matter that the gun jammed. My father turned that gun around to use it as a blunt object and smashed it over my mother's head. I stood there listening to the twanging of the gun bouncing off of her skull.

Twang.

Twang.

He never grew weaker with each blow to her bloody and unrecognizable face. His rage wasn't appeased, and he needed it to leave him. He stood up, and then when I thought he was done, he jumped in the air to land his foot on her throat. Her body, lifeless, just bounced with his force and then rested.

He jumped again.

And again.

After the last jump, he bent over to squeeze her throat and make sure the life had left her.

I realized I could stop him now. I could reach the tower of a man.

I jumped on my father's back as he continued squeezing my mother's throat. I pulled his hair and scratched his eyes. Nothing worked. All the strength I had digging into him wasn't enough. He didn't even know I was there. He stood up with so much force while I was still on his back that I was thrown off into the gravel.

I didn't have time to feel the pain at all. I stood to my feet and saw my mother laying there. I knew she was dead. My mommy was gone, and I had to run.

I ran to the other side of the truck and out a lane that led to another road. I knew my aunt lived not far from there. It was so dark without streetlights to guide me, but I wasn't afraid. I felt like I had been running for so long.

Suddenly, I heard my name being shouted. I stopped in confusion because it was a woman yelling my name. I ran toward the voice. The woman stood outside a big house, and I could see my sister sitting on a bench just inside the front door. I had no idea who this woman was that shouted my name. I didn't care how she knew me. I had one thing on my mind—my mother.

I sat quietly with my sister. We didn't talk about it. I was so cold sitting on the bench that hot summer night. An evening breeze blew through the wet, scarlet t-shirt clinging to my little body. Just twenty minutes before, my t-shirt had been white as snow. Now it was soaked in my mother's blood.

They were afraid I was bleeding, but I was fine. I was shaking but I was alive. I was cold and wet, and I shook. Not the kind of shaking you do when you're nervous. This wasn't like that. This controlled my breathing, and it felt like someone was living in my body. Something moved in and took over every sense I had and made me jerk and shake as if I were having a seizure. I was truly afraid. This was my first encounter with a fear I had never felt before. It moved in and welcomed itself to its new home. Fear evicted any trust I could have had, and it rested in its proverbial recliner. It wasn't going anywhere for a while.

I heard sirens, and a little old lady came down the hall to greet me and my sister. The owner of the home called out and told her to go back to bed and everything was okay. The older woman looked very confused. I'm sure she was. After all, a bloody seven-year-old child was sitting in her foyer shaking like the devil entered her. I'd be confused, too.

I wanted the shaking to stop. It was painful and agitating. I also wanted out of the wet, scarlet t-shirt, but at the same time, I needed it close to me. It was all I had left of my mother, and her blood was all she had to give him to make him stop.

Her debt belonged to me now. I wore it and felt it on my skin. I felt her sins against me, and as sick as it is to say, I needed to keep it.

It was my fault she was gone. I wasn't strong enough to make him stop. I vowed to myself that I would be one day, though. I would be strong enough to protect myself and any woman I saw getting hurt.

I hated him, and I wanted him to be the one laying there. Not my mommy. She loved me and my sisters. In my mind, he never wanted me. He only wanted a son, and I knew it.

If I were a boy, I would have been strong enough. I tried so hard to be that boy. I made myself take as much pain as I could to be strong. I had developed a well-thought-out plan to become strong. I played two summers in a row with my male cousins and my little sister. We played a game that would make me strong like a boy. I would punch them in the stomachs as hard as I could, then they would take a turn punching me. I'll never forget the tightening as my tiny underdeveloped belly knotted into a ball and I fell in a fetal position onto the ground. I'd get up and take another turn. This was a game to them, but not to me. I needed to be strong. I would learn to be strong like a man, but not to hurt people that didn't deserve it. I wanted to help people.

It didn't hurt when my father threw me off his back. I could take it because I was ready. I couldn't pull him off my mommy. I couldn't make him hear me, but I could take it. He was so strong. The hate was stronger. He hated her. I knew he hated her. I think in his mind he thought he had the right to hurt her. He didn't trust her. The feeling was mutual.

It seemed like weeks went by, but in reality, it was only days until I found out my mother was alive! She was okay, and I couldn't believe it. I had never had so many emotions flood through me. During my mother's stay in the hospital, we didn't find out how she was doing until she showed up at the house we were staying at. Everything seemed like a dirty secret. We were a dirty secret.

The man with the kind eyes had been shot with the shotgun three times—once in the middle of his hand, another at the top of his clavicle, and the last shot fired missed his heart by two inches. He made it out of the hospital before my mom did.

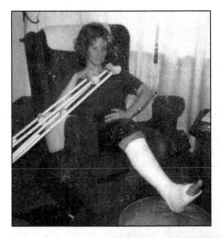

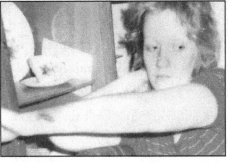

Top left: My mother resting in a chair at the house my sisters and I stayed in while she was in the hospital; Top right: 186 stitches on top of my mother's head; Bottom: The mark on her arm is where the unknown bullet ricocheted and hit.

My mother spent twenty-four hours in a coma. When she awoke, she faced a battered body. Her right leg was broken, and she suffered severe brain damage that wouldn't show until later in her years. She had 186 stitches inside and out of her head. Somehow a fourth bullet had been fired and had ricocheted into her forearm.

My sisters and I temporarily stayed with a relative until my mother was well enough to leave the hospital and figure out what was next for us. I had many relatives, but for whatever reason, my mom's siblings thought this relative was the most stable.

I was more than happy to stay with Dwayne and Karen, and I loved them very much. My heart always desired to do whatever I could to help make others more comfortable. I knew my sisters and I were a nuisance, but at age seven, I was much too small to change the situation. Dwayne and Karen had three children, and they were very well behaved.

Karen had a sweet heart, and I will never forget the bath she allowed me and my sister to take together. The water was so full and way past the level my mom allowed us to have. Karen let us play for what seemed like an hour, and she never yelled at us once. That bath, although so small in the grand scheme of things, was the first time in a long time that I felt the freedom I had felt at my Grammy's house. I even smiled as I pretended to swim and drown out the terrors I had lived through. I can't thank Karen enough for that night of deep waters and freedom.

Dwayne and Karen loved God very much. They seemed honorable, but a severely bitter and religious spirit hid behind the doors of the "holy house." Following the rules as much as possible was a must in their home, and the entire family endured a lot. I'm not sure if some of Dwayne's attitude stemmed from his father's old ways or just the religion rooted deep inside. I know some of Dwayne's father trickled down into his blood. He was not quite like his father, of course, but still a scent remained. It never dawned on me until many years later that condemnation from an iron-fisted religion caused every ounce of heartache. It's easy to replace a relationship with religion when you're told you're never going to be enough for anyone, including Jesus. If you aren't enough and Jesus isn't enough, then nothing is left except earning and deserving your way through life.

There was one day I will never forget. I was playing outside with Dwayne and Karen's son, Isaiah. He wasn't like the other boys I had played with. Isaiah didn't hit me or play rough games. He loved to laugh, and I can still see the biggest smile on his face as his wavy brown hair glinted in the sunlight. He was fun without the bruises, and I liked that.

On this particular day, we had been playing and teasing each other with our glass bottles of soda when I pretended that I was going to spit at him. I didn't spit but wanted to play like I had. Much to my surprise, Isaiah ran and told his dad what he thought I had done. I didn't know how to handle that type of play.

Dwayne called my name with a deep bellow. His voice was like the sounds that the tall man made on an early Sunday morning to his congregation. It was just like the bray on Sunday when there was no clapping or hallelujahs. It was a yell of condemnation, a ridicule yawp. It was deep and sank into my chest like the bass drum did as my immature back pressed against the pews many aching Sundays before.

I was in trouble. I knew this sound. I was well aware of its presence. I walked as quickly as I could just to make my heart stop pounding. I could take it, though. I was getting stronger.

"Did you spit on my son?" Dwayne asked me in a low, deep voice.

"No."

"Well, now you get a beating for spitting and lying, and my boy gets a beating for telling."

I knew in that instant no one would win. Isaiah knew he'd made a terrible mistake for fibbing, and I knew I'd made a terrible mistake for existing.

Dwayne was a big man, and his eyebrows could speak a thousand words had he never said anything at all. There was anger in his eyes. He reminded me of my Grandfather Alastor for a moment. His thick, black brows bent like his, and yet I saw a heart so beautiful in the anger. He really was trying to help teach us. I know now he meant no harm, but my little heart was so broken and wanted mercy, especially for a crime I never committed.

Dwayne told me to pull my pants all the way down to the floor and bend over the bed. I was so embarrassed but had no choice. I complied with his injustice to my little body. He pulled back and struck me with what looked like a yardstick. I wanted to scream, but I knew more was coming. He struck two more times, and then it was the little boy's turn.

I didn't deserve the whipping, and that poor boy didn't deserve one either. I needed to be hugged and loved. I wanted that kind of compassion. Dwayne never understood and only saw punishment as necessary. How could he not see my broken spirit? I was intimate with pain and the procedure of punishment. He didn't abuse me the way his father abused him over and over; however, there were still remnants of law dancing in his eyes.

I cried because I didn't lie. I told the truth. I didn't spit on Isaiah. Plus, I was embarrassed because they saw me naked. Then anger washed over me for the unjust punishment, and I wished I'd spat on Isaiah. I was mentally upside down from witnessing years of terrible abuse, and Dwayne's unkindness and failure to show love fueled my anger.

Dwayne walked me to the kitchen table and made his awful stone-cold face show his brutal strength against a tiny broken child. It wouldn't have taken much to completely break me at this point. I would either burst into tears or scream at the top of my lungs. Only Dwayne's right eyebrow raised when he spoke to me:

"Stop crying."

He made me stop crying and told me to smile. Then he smiled what looked like a genuine smile and told me to go play. I was not permitted to show my hurt. I felt like that was not right, but I didn't know. For a second, I felt like maybe Dwayne was trying to teach me something. I didn't understand at the time, but he was showing me mercy. His father was much, much worse, and this was compassion compared to what Dwayne had endured. His version of punishment and compassion was all he knew and was his way of showing love.

I couldn't help but forgive him, but at the same time, I can honestly say that the smile I gave was such a facade. I wanted the ordeal to be over, and I decided to fake it if I had to. That day was the first time I experienced how to manipulate a human. I did it for myself. At that moment I also knew I needed to be even stronger than I'd ever been. Dwayne showed me that big men weren't strong. They were weak inside and could only be men by overpowering and degrading those smaller in order to maintain control.

Would I grow up to be like Dwayne or my father? I didn't feel that way inside. I felt happy despite it all. I felt like tomorrow could be better, and I was okay. I wondered if Grandfather Alastor ever felt that way. I wondered if he gave up on hope and just accepted what his father before left as his legacy. Grammy said my real and true father was Jesus. She told me that if Jesus was my real Father, then he was my relative. Of course, I didn't understand how I could have a good dad and a bad dad. How could I have a good relative and a bad relative? I wanted all the answers.

The day my mother arrived to pick us up from Dwayne and Karen's house, my sister Jennifer was about to receive the beating of a lifetime. Her crime? Walking in the front yard. She had been forbidden to go out front due to traffic. I'm not sure if a car would have done more damage to her or not. Her pride was wounded.

My mother was frantic, and as beat up as she was, she didn't let all of those stitches in her head, a bullet in her arm, and a broken leg stop her from ranting to Dwayne and Karen how wrong and uncompassionate they were to their relatives.

Mother drove us back to where we had lived before leaving my father so she could figure out what to do next. On that trip, she used her left leg to control the gas and brakes. I remember staring at her cast on her right leg. I remained quiet, though, and didn't ask questions. I knew what had happened. I saw it up close and in person. I saw her leg break on the way down to the pea gravel on the road. It was a quiet ride home, and I needed it to be. There was nothing left to say.

Two injured in shooting outside Scio

A rural Scio man and woman were hospitalized and their assailant transported to the state hospital in Cambridge following a shooting early Sunday near the Scio Auction barn.

Admitted to Timken Mercy Hospital in Canton for treatment of at least three gun shot wounds was ▮▮▮▮▮▮▮▮, who was released from the hospital Tuesday.

Beaten was Janet ▮▮▮▮▮▮, admitted to Twin City Hospital. She was reported in good condition Tuesday.

ARRESTED AND CHARGED with two counts of felonious assault was the woman's 31 year-old husband, ▮▮▮▮▮▮▮▮.

According to the Harrison County Sheriff's office, a call was received about 3:34 a.m. that shots had been fired in the Scio Auction barn lot.

According to authorities, ▮▮▮▮▮▮ fired at ▮▮▮▮ with a rifle and then hit his wife with it. Three young children who were with their mother at the time were unharmed.

Following his arrest, ▮▮▮▮▮ was placed under $40,000 bond, $4,000 cash, by county court judge ▮▮▮▮▮▮▮. The bond was later raised to $60,000 or $6,000 cash.

▮▮▮▮▮▮▮▮ **WAS RELEASED** from the hospital in Cambridge Tuesday and made bond. He is tentatively scheduled to appear in county court at 9:30 a.m. Wednesday.

Newspaper clipping about the shooting

3

Worthless.
Unloved. Abandoned.

Dear Jesus,

I don't want to go to another school. I'm moving, and I'm leaving my yard, my chickens, my tree, and my cats. My dad built the fence for my Appaloosa horse. Her name was going to be Appaloosa Joe, Jesus. He dug all the holes and put the fence posts in. Mommy told me to pray that my daddy doesn't go to prison now. I'm so confused. You did answer my first prayer, though. He's going. I don't understand any of it. Why do I feel so sad? I thought I was supposed to be happy when you answered me, like the day you helped me in the window. This doesn't feel like that day. Mommy says it's for our protection, but she is so sad. She said we are going to a place far away with a swimming pool, and I'm excited about that. It's my favorite thing to do. Okay, I'm so tired, and I have to pack tomorrow. I will pack all my bathing suits. I have five now. Please keep us covered with your precious blood and protect us from the enemy. Let us all sleep good tonight and wake up feeling good in the morning. Watch over Mommy, Daddy, me, Jennifer, and Melissa. In Jesus' name, Amen.

This prayer shows the confusion in my little mind. My mom wanted me to pray that my father would go to prison. Yet, she was so afraid of him that she planned to testify on his behalf—the man that vowed to kill her. I was told to hate him and then told to forgive him and to pray he didn't go to prison. I was so confused. All I wanted was quiet with no more yelling, no more bad words, and no more pain. I didn't want to feel like I was living on the edge of someone else's chaotic mountain.

These little thoughts were mere matches compared to the flame of hate I had built up in my heart. There were so many memories for me to leave behind. Good or bad, these memories were all mine. No matter which way you cut it, my life was about to be a whole lot noisier. Isn't life funny that way? One person might yearn desperately for the sound of children playing and complete chaotic noise to break the silence of their lonely heart, while someone else may desire pure silence to deaden the sound of a broken heart. After all, both broken hearts beat so very differently. Maybe they beat the same, but its pulse is for a different reason.

During the time awaiting my father's trial, my mother hid us in protective houses for battered women. There was no swimming pool awaiting me. There wasn't even a bathtub to pretend I was swimming. There was only a small shower in a large square extending to the ceiling. I'd never seen anything like it before. I remember thinking I could plug the drain, but even if I did, it would only fill an inch.

I knew my mother lied to get me there without a fight. Or

maybe she lied so she could spare herself one more disappointed look on her children's faces. I've never been combative unless necessary, but I don't think I even had the fight left in me at that moment, at least not against my mother. I was saving my fury for the perfect moment. I never complained about our situation for a second because I knew my mother had been through enough.

My mother needed protection from my father. She had placed a restraining order on him the moment she left him to stay with the man with the kind eyes, but my father walked right through it and almost murdered them both. After that, how could she trust a little piece of paper telling my father he legally had to stay away from us? She needed a bodyguard that my father would be inordinately terrified of.

My mother used to tell me and Jennifer a story about Grandfather Alastor's sister. She had a fifteen-year-old son named Christopher who had a real problem with the word "no" and could not stand to be told what to do. One sunny afternoon, Christopher wanted to use his mother's car. She told him she had a hair appointment later that afternoon so he wouldn't be able to use it. Something must have intensely provoked him because the next thing he did was maniacal.

Christopher went to his mother's bedroom, found the pistol she had hidden, and loaded it. Then he walked into the kitchen where she stood beside the refrigerator. He called her name, she turned, and he pointed the gun at her face. She stared into the eyes of a child she once knew, the familiar eyes of her baby boy, as he squeezed the trigger. Her face disappeared into the madness of his contorted mind as he murdered her in cold blood with her own weapon. Christopher was convicted of murder at the age of fifteen and tried as an adult. He was sent to prison until the age of thirty.

My mother decided that she would ask her cousin Christopher to protect us. I remember the first time I met him. He was a gargantuan man with chestnut-colored hair that looked much like the mane of a lion. He was very friendly to me and Jennifer. I would be lying if I said I wasn't a bit taken back as to why my mother thought she could trust a man that murdered his mother in cold blood, but she did. Once again, I knew the truth about him and never said a word. My mother reassured us that this arrangement was only temporary and that he was safe. She told us that he would kill my father if he came within an inch of us. I knew this was a fact because I knew Christopher had done it before.

Then my mother decided that it would be safer to take my father back. She feared he would come after us again, and the running and hiding would get worse until he was locked up. To her, it seemed easier to just stay with him and make him believe everything was going to be okay. (The man with the kind eyes was afraid for his life and no longer wanted to be a part of my mother's broken world.)

I was much too small to know exactly when my dad was going to prison. I knew the time was soon, but I had no idea what day. It felt like I was waiting on Jesus to return like my Grammy said. I wouldn't know the day or hour, only the signs, and they were certainly showing.

I understood that my father was leaving, so while I waited, I played a thousand little scenarios in my head of how life would be without him. I wish I could truly remember all the scenarios that went on in my head. I imagine I played it over and over in my head about how much time I'd get with my mommy. Now I could play with her because she wouldn't have to clean. I may have even smirked when I thought to myself, "No more white glove test." She wouldn't have to stay up all night long and scrub walls or porches or even places nobody ever saw. Surely with him gone, I would have her. She would love to hear me sing, and I wouldn't make her nervous by taking her time. Yes! Yes, I'm certain that was my favorite playback in my mind.

One day per my father's request, we all jumped in the car and went "Gypsy Joe'ing." That was a term my family used when we would go gallivanting in the car. My dad used to call his mom Gypsy Joe because she was always on the go, so I imagine that is why they used the term.

This particular drive wasn't the average Gypsy Joe ride though. This time we had a destination. I had overheard my parents talking about my father not being able to leave the state, but I guess he wanted the satisfaction of breaking the law without anyone other than us knowing it. I remember my father crossing the Ohio state line into West Virginia. He turned the car around in the middle of the road, and my parents started laughing. I laughed away too at the silly escapade with no idea why. We all know how contagious laughs are. I suppose we just needed to take a break from reality and laugh that day.

Two years quickly passed by. Nothing was different at home. It seemed as if nothing had ever happened. That's how it always was, though. My father would mess up, and my mother would clean up the messes he made, just like the times before. It seemed as though what had happened to us all never existed. We never talked about it. Then, something changed.

One morning, my mother woke me and my sister very early. I remember my eyes stinging as she told me to get up. I went downstairs, and she was scurrying in the kitchen as usual while my father sat at his normal seat at the kitchen table. I could feel something thick in the air. Something different was about to happen.

"Today's the day daddy leaves for prison. Three years. Daddy won't be here for three years."

It was time.

My sister started weeping, and I couldn't comfort her. I didn't want to. There was no need to. She needed to be strong, and I couldn't feel, let alone understand, why. I really didn't know how to feel about it all. I had no emotion on my face. I'd prayed in obedience for my mother, and I couldn't stir up any emotion. My lack of emotion was obvious to my father. He saw my face, and he looked at me in disgust.

"Shanda, aren't you even going to cry? Aren't you going to miss me?"

Still nothing.

He kept going on in absolute disappointment as if I weren't hurt enough. He was actually angry at me for not hurting for him! I tried to cry and be sad. I pushed and pushed but couldn't muster a tear. I was starting to think maybe I was happy. I even tried to wince and still there was nothing. Nothing but the smell of bacon and a coward of a man staring at me as if he wished I were never born.

Maybe he saw it on my face that I didn't care because they were taking him. Maybe I didn't care because I was highly trained to move from emotion to emotion without time for a cup of mercy's tea. A child was never meant to stay in stress; no one is meant to stay in a constant state of fear.

I wanted to feel. I really did. I wasn't afraid of him. He couldn't hurt me anymore, and no one could out scream or out whip what he'd done. I was seven, and I had already learned to be numb.

Later that morning, my mother drove us to the place where my father would leave us. He checked in and sat in a chair while policemen scurried around. I hugged him goodbye, and I managed to squeeze a few tears out. I was almost sad. Who knows? Maybe I was so devastated that I didn't know how I was allowed or supposed to feel. I didn't know what was right or wrong anymore. Up to this point everyone had always told me how to act, react, and feel.

All I knew was that I lost my daddy long ago, piece by piece, slap by slap, day by day. I wasn't about to lose my mommy for the second time. I believed she died that day my father tried to take her life. In my mind, I had been preparing to live without a mother. To find out that she lived was the most enrapturing moment of my life. It was almost as if she'd been brought back from the dead. To me, she was. With everything oscillating in my head, I wasn't sure if I was sad about this traumatic life change? Would I miss my father? I don't know. My emotions were as scattered as the memories we all had together. There weren't many, and most were bad.

My mother wasn't a fan of the lonely life. She filed for a divorce shortly after my father went to prison, and it didn't take long for her to date around. She wasn't a fan of belonging to one man either. Who could blame her? She wasn't given much of a choice.

That's when I met him. All the others left before they could meet me in the morning, but he stayed. He wanted to stay. He was handsome but so quiet. I stared at him intently with so much hope. Maybe he would be my new dad.

I danced around the kitchen early that morning trying to make him talk. I put myself on display. If I wanted a new daddy, I had to be sure I played my whole hand. He needed to know how talented I was so that would help him stay. I asked him if he liked to dance and he shook his head no. I thought to myself that this couldn't work. I needed him to have kind eyes, which he did, but I also needed him to talk to me. I needed attention, and I wanted it now. My mother liked him and moved him in immediately, and it wasn't long until she married him.

A couple of years passed by, and I only saw my father a handful of times. My new stepdad would sit in the car while my mother traipsed us up the long sidewalk to enter the prison gates. It only took a couple of visits to unveil the raunchiness of prison life. There were men and women all over the grass on blankets, lip-locked and occupied as they rolled around. Men and women, both young and old, were mauling each other as if my sister and I didn't exist. I was disgusted. I wanted to leave. I felt hot, and my face burned with embarrassment. Still, no one noticed that we were there. My mother and father talked between themselves, and he still didn't notice us after all the time that had passed. As we sat there bored out of our minds, we thought that he didn't seem any different to us.

Me and my sisters at one of the visits with our father.

My mom and stepdad wanted things to change once my father was released. He was supposed to come around every other weekend, and for once I was excited, but not because I wanted to see him—I wanted him to see me. I wanted him to see how great I was doing—without him. I thought for a minute that our relationship could be new. He could be different.

He acted like he wanted to see us. He took us shopping at a store called Hearts. It had toys and clothing for children. I couldn't believe my father was actually taking us shopping. He bought me a small plastic microscope that I was in awe of. I loved it so much. He then took us to one of my favorite pizza places.

He sat awkwardly with us while we ate. I could tell he truly didn't know what to say or do. He started to make strange noises from his mouth that sounded a lot like flatulence. He was laughing, and the noises were getting louder. Jennifer and I started giggling at first, but then I saw young boys at a nearby table staring at us. I was so embarrassed, but I tried to appease my father. I didn't want him to feel any more awkward than we all were already feeling. I laughed along with real tears in my eyes. I wanted to leave so badly. I wanted to hide, and in fact, I slouched in my seat, praying no one would see me there.

After we finished eating, he took us to his mother's house. She was what we called "the mean grandma," but she wasn't really mean. She always had a well-kept home with an aroma of the finest Polish dishes flooding the air. She had a plain face and always wore a moo-moo. She yelled a lot and had a potty mouth. She wasn't soft or kind. She never shaved her armpits or legs, which made Jennifer and I giggle and wonder why. (She once told us that God put hair there for a reason.) She was in no way a "grammy." She just showed us love in a different way.

When we pulled in her driveway, all the childhood memories washed over me. It was as if the air had returned to the lungs of a drowning child. I gasped but tried to hide it. I saw the long, bumpy sidewalk where Jennifer and I put endless miles on a tricycle for two. The sappy trees and smell of pine never smelled so good.

I was nervous to see her, so wanting to make conversation with my father, I asked him if she would be happy to see us because I hadn't seen her in almost three years. During all my racing thoughts, I didn't realize that I called her by her real name.

My father, once again in a defeated and disappointed voice, said, "Shanda...call her Grandma. That will hurt her feelings."

"Her feelings!" I thought. "You have got to be kidding me. When...when...when...when would they care about my feelings?"

I almost wish he had yelled at me. He spoke so softly as if

he too was reminded of all he'd lost. I felt awful because I didn't mean to hurt him. My father didn't realize that, since my sisters and I had not seen our grandmother for years, we were not used to calling her "Grandma." That name felt foreign. To me, she was no grandma, only a person I once knew. A memory.

I thought this walk down memory lane would feel good, but it didn't, and that made me furious. I thought spending time with my father and reuniting with my grandparents would pick up where we left off. It didn't. It was as if my father was introducing his newly adopted, older children to two of the most unwelcoming, emotionless people I'd ever met. It was clear we were not welcome. They looked at us as if we had three heads. I just wanted to leave. The more I thought about leaving, the more I wanted to punish my father. I also wanted to punish them all. His whole family deserved to feel my pain because they all abandoned us. They hadn't tried to contact us at all to my knowledge. I felt so unwanted in such a familiar place. I didn't know how to react. I felt as if I belonged there but didn't deserve it. I felt as if I'd sinned, and they all knew it.

A memory popped into my head of my grandmother's shrill voice waking me up in the car.

"Quit leaning on the door, you stupid son of a b——! You'll fall out!"

I'm sure you know the whole word she exclaimed. That's what she called all her grandchildren, and I wasn't any more special than the others. I wish I could tell you that it startled me and made me cry. Unfortunately, it was just part of normal conversation at my grandmother's. We were always called names. Stupid, dumb, fat, worthless, and so many more come to mind.

I was no longer excited to see her at that point. My father showed us his new camper where he planned to stay until he found a job and bought a home. I endured the visit, but part of me felt so empty. I was surrounded by hopelessness, and I couldn't shake it.

My father's visits became fewer and fewer over time. He stopped showing up, and on his second to the last visit, he told me I looked like a slut in my skirt. I was a skinny, long-legged, knobby-kneed girl. Everything looked short on me. But he had to make sure I knew what he thought about me. My thought was what made him think he had the right to give his opinion about me. I know he was my father by birth, but he hadn't been a dad to me in years.

He came one more time after he called me a slut, but not to see me and my sisters. I moseyed into the living room and sat with my stepdad. I kept peeking into the kitchen to see if my father noticed me roughhousing with my stepdad. I wanted to make my father jealous. He never reacted. I felt as if I were staring at a man in a casket waiting for his chest to rise and fall. There was no life detected. I started shrieking in laughter, and still no response. The aroma of death was all that remained in that room. He got up and left our home.

I walked into the kitchen and my mother said that my father wouldn't be coming back to visit us. He was going to marry my mother's cousin. Once again, I didn't understand what I did wrong. This abandonment was a punishment so big. Bigger than the screams. Undeserved.

My father's leaving reminded me of the time he hit his head on the basement door frame while exiting the basement. He knew it was there, and it had always sat low. He had been chasing me and my sister to swing at us, so he had to blame someone.

"Get the h— out of the way, you stupid sons of b——s!"

The blame was never his. We were as good as anyone to abuse just as long as he didn't take the blame. As long as someone was there to take the blow, all was well with the world.

Now he had rejected us once again.

Words whispered in my heart—Worthless. Unloved. Abandoned.

Before my father walked out of our lives, my mother received permission for Bill, my stepdad, to adopt us. I was so happy yet so destroyed all at the same time.

I couldn't cry. I could only hate. I hated my father for hurting me. I hated him for leaving me. I hated him for wanting me to want him more than he could ever want me. I hated him and all he ever was. He never wanted me, and I knew it. This time I really knew it. But he wasn't gone for forever, though. He didn't live far from where we lived, and it was impossible to live in a small town and never run into one another. I saw him several times out and about and quite a few times in nearby grocery stores. After making quick eye contact, he would look away as if he didn't see me. He tried to hide in the aisles so he wouldn't have to face me. I guess he wanted to hide his shame and pretend things never happened. I would giggle under my breath watching him shuffle around each corner, but at the same time, I was still very heartbroken at the fact he was literally hiding from me.

I never showed my anger or emotion for fear of anyone

thinking I didn't want my new dad to adopt me. I was truly happy that he wanted me and my sisters. He was so amazing and loved us for no reason. He accepted us for no reason. He wanted to raise us for no reason. He never said he wanted a boy. We were enough to him, and that was an all-new feeling to my young heart.

My stepdad Bill with my mom

My new dad had two other little girls, and I was so excited to meet them. For a short time, his oldest daughter came to stay with us. I loved hanging out with her since she was only three months older than I was. We had our spats, but I adored her.

One time, my stepsister's mother wanted Bill, my new dad, to buy my stepsister shoes. While buying shoes was not an unreasonable request by itself, this greedy woman was still receiving child support for a child that lived with us, not her. My parents thought it wasn't fair for them to purchase the shoes because the mother received the money to buy such items. Plus, Bill didn't have the extra money because everything we had went to pay his child support.

Bill and my stepsister's mother had a terrible argument on our front lawn. Of course, watching the argument made my stepsister feel awful about even asking for new shoes. I've never seen such a greedy woman in the flesh. When Bill refused to buy the shoes, she took my stepsister home with her, and, poof, she was gone from our lives. After that terrible fight, Bill never pursued visitation and just quietly paid his child support.

Bill was a soft-spoken man who wanted nothing to do with his haughty ex-wife. The less fighting, the better was his idea of keeping the peace. He'd been hurt and didn't want to deal with it anymore even if that meant not fighting for his children. Little did he realize that his children felt exactly like I felt—their father abandoned them to another family.

They say there are two sides to every story. Let's just say our family story was more than I could keep track of. I say ours was a rhombicosidodecahedron. But here we were. We were a brand new family, and I was thirteen years old with a new name.

After receiving the news of what my biological father did to his family, the coal mine fired him. We had nothing. My new father Bill owed over twenty-thousand dollars in child support, and after we did the math of how much he owed and how long it would take to pay off, I would be eighteen when it was paid and over with. I knew this all too well because my mom made sure my sisters and I knew. She wanted us to know so we understood. Plus, when the answer "no" is all we heard, she wanted us to see why.

From the time I was born until I was eighteen years old, we moved house-to-house thirteen different times. We were always hopping from job to job and from school to school. I didn't stay long enough at any school to make many friends. I felt like an

Playing outside at one of the schools I attended. I was so ashamed of the way I looked that I couldn't even smile for a photo.

outcast to everyone I met. And the more we moved, the poorer we became. There were many times we stood in the lines for food at the food pantry.

Anyone could see we were poor; I most definitely looked the part. I wore an oversized boy's winter jacket because we shopped at the Salvation Army store. My hair was long in the back and grown out in the front from the lack of grooming.

I used to be so pretty. I used to look so pretty. I used to feel so pretty. I wonder if I wanted that memory gone more than any of the others. Knowing and not being able to change anything is a dagger in the heart. To me, I was an ugly, poor, and embarrassed girl. Every day of school was like walking naked through the hallways. I could feel them staring at me. They could see every ounce of shame I had lived and I couldn't hide it anymore.

There was one thing I had though—Bill—and he chose us on purpose. He reminded me of how Jesus loved me. I loved Bill immediately because he made it easy to do. He started to open up after some time had passed. He was actually fun, and he showed me something that I'll never forget. He could dance.

Yes, that first morning we met he had denied being able to dance, but he could definitely dance. He was absolutely incredible. I couldn't believe it. I watched him sway to the beat and keep rhythm like no man I'd ever seen. As he danced, I thought back to when I had asked if he could dance. Now he trusted me, and I smiled inside. I watched intently until I could mimic his every move. I showed him I could dance like him, and he and my mom were amazed.

As time passed, Bill started becoming more than a friend to me and my sisters. He was becoming a true father. He shared stories with us about his life before he married my mother. He told us that they had met in high school, had always liked each other, but never pursued a relationship. But more important than his stories, we started making new memories as a family. The smallest things in life can mean so much.

Bill loved bacon and mustard sandwiches. Every time he ate one, my sisters and I cringed and told him how disgusting that was. He challenged me to try it, and I reluctantly took a bite. I absolutely loved it. Today, that is the only way I eat a bacon sandwich.

Then we have those colossal memories that are so huge and so funny that they are hard to tell because it takes everything in you to squeeze out words between the laughter. One morning, that we will never forget, a shrill banshee cry filled the air.

"Bat!"

There is something about that small, three-letter word that can cause a mighty fortress to crumble as hysteria swoops in. Bats are a tiny, blind creature, but we react worse than they do. All they want is out of the house and away from the chaos. On the other hand, our house was instantly terrorized, but not by the bat. The real mania was caused by four females in distress. We all swarmed together, running room to room, as Bill tried chasing the poor little bat. We were in my mother and stepdad's room when suddenly my mother screamed at the top of her lungs.

"It's under my nightgown!"

Lo and behold, that little bat flew straight up my mother's pajamas. As it slapped its wings against the flesh of her legs, she launched herself into the air colliding with the closet door. There was a sound like a great thunderclap, and the door was no more. Directly after the bat evacuated my mother's pajamas, it flew up the stairs and into my room. I stood in the middle of the living room waiting to see if Bill was going to catch the bat. The next thing I saw was unforgettable.

The bat flew down the stairwell, past me, and into the dining room. Bill wasn't far behind, but when he started down the stairs, I couldn't believe that it was my stepdad. He looked like he was wearing a full-length burqa. He had wrapped a large blanket around his head, and the blanket covered his entire body down to the floor. In one hand he held a badminton racket, and, in the other hand, he had a lawn rake.

The bat mindlessly flew past my head once again with my stepdad hot on its trail. Back up the stairs they went, and the chase continued.

I heard Bill let out a yell and saw him start down the stairs, only this time the bat was chasing him. Then Bill slipped on his makeshift burqa blanket and lost his footing. He stiffened his entire body like a statue as he tried balancing himself on the edge of a step. His eyes widened as he teetered back and forth, unsure if he would be able to hold it together and keep from plummeting to the bottom of the stairs. He had a death grip on his misemployed weapons of choice as the crafty bat circled him once more and flew back up the stairs. Bill redirected himself with a quick swivel of his stiff-as-a-board body and hightailed it back up the few steps he had nearly fallen down.

Then we heard a whack from the badminton followed by dead silence. I stood there afraid to move.

My mom yelled from her room, "Did you kill it?"

Not a word was said.

We heard footsteps walking across the floor above our heads. We all huddled in the living room waiting. Bill started down the stairs, and he was carrying a blanket with the small bat wrapped inside. He smiled as he proudly walked past us.

"I stunned it," he said.

He put the unconscious bat in a safe place where neither the bat nor people would come in contact with each other. I will never forget the day that a bat lost to a man in a blanket.

Our memories as a family increased as time moved on. We were a real family, and for a split second, I thought of my first father. I thanked him in my heart where no one but God and I could hear. I thanked him for a new life and a new chance. It didn't matter that I was poor. I'd never let my mother know how I felt inside and how I was insecure and afraid of so many things. She was too precious to me, and I'd never let her see.

I overheard my mother tell a few friends about that terrible night in that dank town. She told them she was shot for her kids and how she had taken a beating for us many times. I was mortified. It had been my fault, and I'd never forgive myself.

All I could do after overhearing my mother was surrender my life to her and do whatever she asked. She assured me that, when our times got tough, hers were far tougher than I had ever experienced, and I shouldn't complain. I understood. She made sense to me in those moments. She'd been through far too much with her own father and then my biological father. Anytime I had a concern or questioned anything, she often referenced her childhood and her life with my first father. She would use those memories to tell me I shouldn't talk back or treat her poorly. It worked. I felt disgusting as a human, and I didn't want to ask her for anything.

My mother's disappointed look of being unable to give me something was far worse than having nothing at all. I remember a time when I wanted to go to cheer camp so badly. I heard my mother and Bill talking about the finances, and I knew that I wasn't going to go well before I asked. Those little things slowly wore me down. They eroded me and scraped me away on the inside, but I'd never show it to my family, especially my mother. She'd been through enough. I owed her my life, and I would never tell her about the tormentors that haunted my head. I tucked them away ever so nicely in my closet of secrets, a dark, unwanted place to hide away all that did me harm. They lived with all the regrets and sad moments of my life.

When our finances became even worse than before, I watched my mother eat popcorn. At first, I thought she loved it because she ate so much of it, but then I overheard her tell Bill that there wasn't much food and that was her way of making ends meet even though the popcorn was ripping her stomach apart. I felt so guilty for eating regular food while she ate popcorn for meals. I couldn't continue eating if my mom was bleeding internally from malnutrition. The kernels were cutting her insides just like guilt was cutting mine. So, I started eating popcorn with her. She asked me why and I told her I would not eat until she did. And I didn't.

Sadly, my dedication to my mother and eating only popcorn was the start of a long, dangerous journey for me. I started developing anorexia around the age of eleven. I had no idea what I was doing to my body and wouldn't know anything until many years later.

My mother noticed that I'd do anything for her. She knew I woke up in the middle of the night and quietly scurried through the house cleaning. She'd wake up and be so proud of me. I made them breakfast in bed and coffee in the morning. She gloated to all her friends and family how amazing I was. She would talk not only about how helpful I was but also about how great of a dancer and singer I was. I could mimic anyone. I could create a crowd of people around me in less than one song. She built me up so high that I wondered if I failed her, what would happen? I decided I just couldn't let that happen. I had to work harder.

✸

In the dark shadows of Satan's schemes, where he hides our shame and helps us fade away, was another saddened and very lonely little girl. My sister Jennifer was trying to feel the warmth of her big sister's limelight. She only wanted a little, and I knew. I saw her hunger for attention and acceptance. I wanted to keep her safe, not necessarily from others but from our own mother. How could I help them both? My mother had no idea what was happening to Jennifer's spirit. Jennifer was so broken-hearted because she never felt loved or wanted—denied by her father and now her mother.

Neither my biological father nor my mother ever meant to deny us affection of any kind. They tried to live the American Dream, but it was more a replica of an American nightmare. I know my mother never intentionally tried to treat any of her daughters differently, but it was happening. Because Jennifer wasn't like me, our mother interpreted Jennifer's never wanting to help her or fuss over her as meaning Jennifer didn't love her. That was never the case, but that's how our mother saw it.

Jennifer was different as an individual, and I loved that about her. She had ached inside for affection for years. She was a little overweight and would battle that demon all her life. People were so heartless to her including children at school who spat on her. She was another reason I fought many fights. I protected her. I loved her so much, and she had a heart so big for a world that treated her as dirty as the secrets we kept.

As I watched my mother love us throughout the years, it was like watching a child reach for a parent in desperation to be held, and heartlessly the parent walks away. Don't get me wrong, my mother loved us the best way she knew how. She was taught to love with conditions, not affection and attention. I knew she loved us because I heard her defend us in many arguments with many people on many occasions. She'd stick up for us even if we were wrong. She could say what she wanted about us, but no one else would ever have that right.

Little did my mother or father know, but something was being created. As children do, Jennifer and I learned quickly and became a product of our environment. Two monsters were created, and no one could have stopped that creation. One monster, uncherished, withdrawn, and desolate, bound to live a life dying to be connected to love and to be loved in some way. The other monster would live only for an endless cycle of feeding a man-pleasing spirit. Neither could be happy. Neither could be appeased. Loved or unloved, no matter the reason, we would only wish to be forever the other sister. Jennifer wanted to feel thin and understood. I wanted to be Jennifer to fight my way to the top for her. I begged God to help her. I begged God to make her skinny because I thought that would make her happy. I wanted God to help her bravely stand out in her own light. Her heart was so big and I wanted the world to see it. This sublunary world never deserved her or any of her attention, but she craved its acceptance so desperately.

4

My Goodbye

Dear God,

I've been told that the year 2000 is all there is. We will be no more after that. I'm told not to be mad at you, but I am. I'm fourteen and I wanted to get married and have children someday. You made me for such a time as this and I'm so angry. My mom and stepdad are not saved, and we are now C and E Christians. Christmas and Easter are the only times we really go to church. Grammy and Grandpa Bill quit going because the church hurt them so badly. They don't want to be a part of that strict religion. I still have a desire to be close to you. I miss you so much, but you are like a memory to me. Certain times when the seasons change, I think of you. Since I won't live past the age of twenty-three, I need to be saved. I know it will be hard alone in school and in my home, but I don't care. The church I went to said I need evidence and that evidence was speaking in other tongues. So, I'm begging you to help me to do it. I can't cry any more tears than I am. I can't thank you any longer or hit this floor any harder! Don't you hear me? Am I just another one of your lost causes? Fine! I'm done! You don't even want me anymore. I'm used up, and I can't even please you...

Sadly, that was my prayer to be saved. I begged God with all I had. I sat there all alone on my bedroom floor begging God for forgiveness. I begged God, and because I didn't speak in the holy tongues the church said I needed to, I just gave up. I quit trying to seek him out. I quit trying to be better, and all my hope was ripped away. All my heartache about God was a lie. He wanted me back, but because of a religion, I truly believed he rejected me.

I couldn't imagine how a God so big could allow a starry-eyed girl with a tear-soaked face to stay all alone with her imagination of desolation. He was so quiet that I could have heard a pin drop. I waited so long on that hard floor that my legs fell asleep. I finally wiped my face, dusted my knobby knees off, and set my face like flint. I was angry. I was done. I decided that I would have a life as fast as I possibly could.

I never could have lived up to my impractical idea of God. This God of nonsensical laws and regulations was a hard man to me. I already had long hair and thought that's what it took. I was truly marked, but not by an unreachable God. I was marked by an impossible law made by man.

If only I knew then what I know now, I would have had the faith that Jesus died for me and my works were not necessary at all. Religion was already sentencing me to hell. Do this and do that to make sure you are saved, they all told me. If I had so much "to do," then why did he die? Paul was clear—"There are diversities of gifts, but the same Spirit. There are differences of ministries, but the same Lord. And there are diversities of activities, but it is the same God who works all in all. But the manifestation of the Spirit is given to each one for the profit of all: for to one is given the word of wisdom through the Spirit, to another the word of knowledge through the same Spirit, to another faith by the same Spirit, to another gifts of healings by the same Spirit, to another the working of miracles, to another prophecy, to another discerning of spirits, to another different kinds of tongues, to another the interpretation of tongues. But one and the same Spirit works all these things, distributing to each one individually as He wills." (I Corinthians 12:4-11)

I wasted so much time not believing that God was enough. I squandered the only thing a man can never buy—time. I wasted time being Martha. I worried what it all looked like from the outside in and never thought about what was occurring on the inside. I wondered if I'd ever be enough.

Not every anamnesis is torture. I can recall quite a few jovial memories. I will never forget the day I asked Bill if I could drive his five-speed Subaru car. He often allowed me to shift the gears from the passenger seat, so I thought I was ready to get behind the wheel. It seemed easy enough. I knew how to keep a car on the right side of the road and now felt comfortable enough to shift the gears at the same time. So, off we went. Me in the driver's seat, my mother sitting in the backseat, and Bill in the passenger seat reciting directions in a calm, soothing voice.

However, there was one tiny and very important detail Bill forgot to mention and I never thought to ask about. He assumed I had enough sense and had watched him long enough to know better. I was slowly going along an old back road not far from our house and was about to shift into second gear. Instantly, it hit me.

What in the world was I supposed to do with a clutch? Do I push the clutch all the way down or just push lightly as I do with the brake? In fear of slamming my parents' heads against the dash and back seat, I lightly tapped the clutch.

The car growled and made noises as if it were going to either eject me from its presence or eat me alive. My eyes opened wide in panic as I experienced what happens when you have no right to be behind the wheel of a car at the age of thirteen. Chaos surrounded me, and the commotion resonated throughout the car. I heard my mother screaming in hysterics in the backseat and fearing for her life.

"Dear Jesus!" I thought. "We're going to die."

My stepdad started laughing loudly, but all I could focus on were roars from the angry car. Bill tried to calm me down because, at this point in the madness, I had now lost my ability to drive. The pressure was debilitating me. Bill took the wheel and directed me when to push the clutch all the way to the floor. My hands were holding the sides of my face as I tried to regain composure. Then I looked in the rearview mirror and realized there now was a car behind me.

"Oh, my God in heaven, save us!" I shrieked.

At this point, my mother was laying down on the back seat in sheer embarrassment, and Bill, well, he was laughing himself into tears. I finally started to see our house up ahead. All I could think about was how many promises I was going to owe to God if we made it out alive.

There it was. Home. Still panicking, I whipped the wheel from Bill's hands and drove the car three inches from the stop sign near our driveway. I slammed on the brakes. Suddenly, all was silent. I stared out the front of the car breathing as if I had run a marathon.

My mother slowly poked her head up hoping it was all over. As she lifted herself back into a normal seated position, I noticed her hair looked like she had just landed out of the belly of a tornado. It was standing straight up as if it, too, was scared for its life. I started to wonder what she had been doing back there. She must have been thrashing throughout the car the entire time. Bill sat there quietly with tears from laughing so hard rolling down his face. I could only sputter out two words in a monotone voice, "Never again."

It took a few months for me to be able to laugh about that day. Now, I can't help but giggle every time I see a stick shift. My stepdad had more faith in me than I realized. Or perhaps he just knew he could keep me safe as long as he was by my side. He was always trying to teach me new things, even if it meant getting out of my comfort zone.

By the time I was fifteen, my mother was known as the mom that all the teens wanted to hang out with. She liked to make them feel at home and thought it was okay to let them all use our place for a party spot. Now, as an adult woman, I really think it was mere attention that my mother desperately sought out. Maybe she just wanted to feel needed, even if it were by a few dunderheaded teenagers. Her desire for simply being loved and appreciated is what set my life on its next trajectory.

I specifically remember her coming to pick me up from my friend's house one day with an eighteen-year-old named Adam in the vehicle. I knew him from my high school, and I hated him because he would make up insane reasons to hurt my feelings. He was the school jock and made fun of me for having a boy as my best friend. He made fun of my body all the time because he thought I had small breasts. He told all his high school jock friends that I had small breasts and I was sleeping with my best friend. Kids can be so cruel, but as someone who was about to graduate, he knew better.

I had met my best friend in fifth grade and am now certain that God sent him to me. He was truly my only real friend in life at that time. I loved my best friend, and I was a virgin. He and I were simply friends and had never crossed that line. Adam made both me and my friend so uncomfortable. My best friend's older brother hung around Adam, so it made it difficult to escape his taunting.

So, there I was looking at this contemptibly obnoxious block-head in my mother's car. Soaked from swimming, I got in the car and scowled at Adam while asking my mother why he was in the car. I spoke as if he couldn't hear me, but clearly he could. He smiled with an ornery grin as if to flirt with the idea that my mother liked him more than me.

Adam started coming around a lot to spend time with my mom and dad. The more he came around, the more he gave the cockiest impression that he liked me. He was so arrogant; I couldn't stand him, yet I was attracted to him.

The idea that the most popular guy in school would ever like someone like me made me feel special. He was prom and home-coming king. He was perfect, and I was not. He was brassy, yet his vulgarity was unrecognizable to me. I was accustomed to that environment and couldn't be offended even if someone had been paid to try. My mother seemed fine with the absurd idea that we date each other.

Adam had feverishly plotted to have me, and no one saw it coming. I can only look back now and see a bright-eyed, innocent, blonde girl, blind as a bat, jumping too far into deep waters. My discernment of him had been on point. I knew not to jump. I knew it was never meant to be. I wanted to be smart, but I needed to be reckless. After all, God had abandoned me, and I'd only live to be twenty-three, so I needed to act fast. I knew what was happening in my mind, and I needed someone to stop me. I had a way of thinking like no child I'd ever seen then or now.

People often ask, "What goes on in the mind of a child?" I remember.

I wanted to feel love and be loved.

I wanted to see myself dancing in someone else's eyes who didn't want to look away in disgust.

I wanted to be wanted on purpose.

I wanted to show the world I was strong enough to take on anything. Anyone was allowed to try, and I would allow anyone to show up for the challenge.

Or maybe I just didn't know my true worth. My worth was decided by everyone and anything but God.

The world screamed "Prove yourself, child!" And I tried. It still rings in my head from time to time. I was already being formed by a world that I myself was made to form. I was made to shape and have dominion over it. I now thought and reacted as it commanded me to.

Remember the popcorn dinners I ate with my mother so she

wouldn't feel alone in her sacrifice for the family? That's just one example of my insane thought process. Here's another: My mother was a smoker, and I asked her to quit smoking. She swore it was impossible to quit, so I told her that I'd start smoking with her, become addicted, and then show her it was possible to quit. That idiotic idea was no different than my trying to live inside my sister's head to fight for her. I was picking battles that never belonged to me. I wanted to fight for something. I never wanted anyone to feel what I'd felt. I'd fight the way I wanted someone to fight for me.

I would have fought for God, but he wasn't noisy enough or fast enough at responding to me. I desired a reaction. I needed immediate answers. Oh, the man-pleasing spirit was growing at rapid speeds, and I kept it well fed.

So, back to my story about the high school jock. I made my choice and dated him for three long, painful years. It was hell, but I wanted to prove that I could make Adam love me. I wanted people to stand around in awe of the girl who tamed the untamable. Then they could see there was something special about me. I wanted them to see that I was different. One thing was true—I was different.

All my friends warned me that Adam was a cheat and a liar. I'll never forget my English teacher/school counselor pulling me out of my first period class to beg me to break up with him. The teacher warned me about the time this boy dated two sisters at once. My response? I told the teacher that I was only dating him, and I actually said, "It's not like I am going to marry him."

I wish I could go back, much like we all want to go back and reason with ourselves. What would I tell me? I'd say, "Shanda, first of all, God hears you. God is two things you need. He is Power, and he is Love. Powerful enough to destroy anything in his path, which is why you are attracted to this silly man-child. However, God is also Love. The man-child knows nothing of love. You need both power and love to survive this relationship." Yes, that is what my older self would say to my younger self. Of course, younger me would never listen. I'd hear nothing about God or reason regardless of how much I needed it.

Not long after my conversation with my teacher, I received a letter from New York City. A modeling agency wanted a few headshots of me! I wanted to be a model, and I planned to go to New York. About the same time that I received the letter, more news came along. I was pregnant. I was seventeen, and my plans were falling right into place. I would have a family before I was twenty-three and the world ended.

My family was ecstatic and started planning right away. Adam's mother was not so impressed by our carelessness. I wanted a baby, though. I had told Adam that if we became pregnant by June, we could have the baby in the middle of both of our birthdays. We had it all figured out. Until my first doctor's appointment.

At what was supposed to be an exciting doctor's appointment, the doctor sat me down and told me I had precancerous cells. Along with the scary "C" word, I was told it was because I had HPV. This could only mean one thing—Adam had cheated on me. The doctor said I would have to have a colposcopy and a biopsy to see what stage I was in. These procedures went on every month, and many biopsies followed. Several times after the biopsies, I lived through the horror of thinking I was losing my baby due to bleeding.

As if being pregnant and hearing the "C" word wasn't enough,

Adam accused me of cheating on him. He was guilty, and he was hoping I was, too. He knew I wasn't. He only hoped I was so he could ease the torment inside his own mind. His evil accusation should have awoken what human heart I had left, but it only deepened its slumber. I remained quiet. I never said a word. I was taken back to the day my father left for prison. I was quiet and numb. Accused and punished.

I knew then, with a baby in my belly and a broken heart in my chest, that this was only the beginning of the hell I'd laid out so perfectly for myself. As goal oriented as I was, I realized that I had bitten off way more than I would ever be able to chew. I was having a baby with a man who cheated on his pregnant girlfriend, and I was enduring multiple biopsies because of his little rendezvous. He came forward several months later and admitted the affair, along with giving me the curse of his unfaithfulness. My journey was only beginning.

Then Alec was born. And there I was with an eight-pound, fourteen-and-a-quarter-ounce bouncing baby boy. I loved this boy more than anything I had ever loved. I would stare at him for endless hours watching him breathe. I was suddenly afraid of everything in life. I found myself crying, scared to death all because his dried-up umbilical cord was hanging on by a hair. Oh, the ridiculousness of the matter. He was all I now lived for.

I suppose I was still living with the idea that I could help Adam also. My new son and I would wait for hours that turned into days for a phone call. Eventually, Adam would call with an excuse of some sort as to why he couldn't come to see me and my newfound love. I found out numerous times that he was with another woman

or out on a boat some-
where with several women
at a time. The phone would
ring in the middle of the
night with calls from random women, but I still
believed him. Even though
he lied over and over, I was
always the one apologizing.
He would manipulate me
into being an accuser and
then tell me how wrong
it was for me to accuse an
innocent man.

Me at 17 years old holding Alec

While I watched my baby sleep, I cried for Alec, my son. My
tears fell like all the promises Adam and many others made to me.
All the while I thought to myself, "How could anyone not want
to spend time with this angelic being?" He was so beautiful, and I
knew he'd love me more than Adam ever could. I made a promise
to Alec that day in my heart that I would never tell him that his
daddy wouldn't show. But what was a promise anyways? No one
had ever kept one for me. Every lie told to me became another
brick in a wall surrounding my broken heart. I hid behind it, and
that wall was strong. I trusted no one, and I let every man know it.

I was told that most men needed to sow their wild oats, and
surely Adam would love only me after all I had given up. My modeling career, my heart, and my youth were given to a man-child
who would show me that most men were cowards. I wanted Adam

so badly to be the man my real father never could be. I even conjured up some imaginary relationship that only existed in my own world. Then I let Adam woo me into marriage.

There was one thing that was true—I was so sorry. I was sorry that I lost myself. I was sorry that I let someone hurt me. I was sorry I had nothing left to give. The only thing that remained was the grin on his face just like the many I'd seen before. That evil, sickening grin that lured me in was engraved into my soul. It was a silent mockery of me. I was its last laugh, and its biggest joke was on me.

For years, I lived with lie after lie and sin after sin. The pornography addiction became worse, and the truth was seeping out of his sin bucket. He tried to hide it several times, but he kept getting caught. I stayed in this trap because he told me the truth after I pried it out of him. To me, it made sense to forgive him since he told me the truth, and I guess as long as you told the truth, you could do whatever you like. That only pertained to him, of course.

We had decided to have no more children after our first son. In my heart of hearts, I was afraid to have any more children with a man with so many illnesses. My biggest concern was keeping my child safe. So we decided Adam would have a vasectomy. However, four short months after his procedure, I was pregnant. The strangest thing about the entire situation was that some of my family, friends, and even my doctor accused me of having an affair. The only person that didn't was my husband. I was so sure he would ask for a paternity test, but even after all the accusations, he didn't.

Maybe he was hoping I had cheated, too. My potential guilt could free him from the hands of his mind drowning him in the well of his own guilt. He went back to the doctor that did the procedure and found out he needed to have another. For a moment I actually felt bad for him, but only for a moment.

When this little bundle of a surprise arrived, there was no denying he was his father's son. He was a whopping seven pounds and a half ounce. I could not have thanked God any more for not letting me get in the way of this amazing gift. I knew he had a great purpose. No man could stop him from entering the world. He was a ball of energy and fire. It was no wonder that his hair was red. That feisty spirit fit just right with his fiery hair. The thought still ran fervently through my mind that I was in deep now and with two small boys to boot. I had to stay and make myself strong enough to take the abuse.

Abuse has many faces. I was introduced to the mental side of things. It was never physical, and Adam was a lot of things, but physically abusive was not one of them. So, to me, his not being physically abusive was enough to keep our marriage together. I thought I was doing much better than my mother because I wasn't black and blue. Instead, my bruises were hidden and tucked away. I was thankful that my boys would never see what I went through.

However, I wasn't aware of what was happening to my boys mentally after catching their father with pornography he had hidden everywhere throughout the house. I felt in my spirit that Adam was hiding it, but I could never find it. He hid it in the dressers beneath the drawers, and he cut little pictures out of books and placed them inside the tops of the door frames. He would tell the boys to cover their eyes during R-rated movies he watched while I was working. I had no idea that their tiny little minds were being formed into possible replicas of their father. I knew he was sick, and there was so much more to this need for porn.

❄

Since I grew up learning about Jesus from Grammy, I knew our little family needed to go to church. We needed to go to Jesus, not just the building. So many people make it sound like the building will save you once you're inside. Perhaps the sanctuary is the holy place, but what if Jesus doesn't dwell there? Then, the building is as empty as the hearts of the Pharisees.

We attended a church exactly like the one I went to as a child. We paid our tithes faithfully, we wore our "holy attire" every day, and I never wore a drop of makeup while attending that church. We were accepted as long as we obeyed the rules. Some churches tell you they won't judge you, but try to be a leader or join in on the reindeer games and see what happens and what choices you have.

When we entered the building that first Sunday, the women were drab and sad looking with long, dried-out hair wrapped around into some of the largest buns I'd ever seen. The women my age and older were dressed as if their great-grandmother's closet had vomited all over them. Some of the younger ladies wore tight pencil skirts, colorful blouses, and stilettos. Perhaps their attire was forgiven because they were in school, and of course, their parents were just happy they were wearing a skirt at all. All the men were dapper and fresh. Most were clean-shaven, but this only revealed the grimaces they made at their wives if they stepped out of place.

Me wearing an oversized shirt and no makeup and showing off my long "glorious" hair

This church environment was comforting to me in a sick and demented way, and either way you cut it, it was discipline, and we needed a few rules in our lives.

I joined the choir immediately, and I loved singing for God. My only lack was I wasn't singing to God. I was only singing for him. There is quite the difference. Worship is a form of sacrifice, but I wasn't giving my singing to God, though. I was doing it merely because I had never been taught what true worship was. Singing "for" God is a great way to help encourage others and lift one's spirit. However, singing "to" God breaks down walls and barriers.

For example, the idea of "Send Judah first" comes from 2 Chronicles 20:21. The Hebrew word for Judah is yä·dä meaning "to give thanks, laud, praise." Send praise first! After Jehoshaphat consulted with the people, he appointed men to sing to the Lord and to praise him for the splendor of his holiness as they went out at the head of the army, saying: "Give thanks to the LORD,...

for his love endures forever" (Psalm 136). Those men always went ahead of the army. This was faith before action!

I lacked faith and had no idea. I'm not sure if anyone in our church truly understood what faith was and what the Bible truly taught about the Christian life. All they ever preached on were end times, tithes, women's clothing, and Acts 2:38. Once in a while, a man would get called out from the pulpit. I'll never forget the time it happened to me.

Before church started that Sunday, I told my pastor that someone asked me why I didn't cut my hair. I happily told my pastor that I let that person know it was "against my religion." I didn't even know what that phrase meant, but I thought my pastor would be proud. After all, I was "defending the gospel" or so I thought. During his sermon, the pastor, with a disgusted look on his face, spoke of how we needed to be mindful of what we say to people and how we sound like a cult when we use the terminology "against my religion."

My countenance changed, and I remember feeling hot and embarrassed. Why wouldn't he have said that to my face? He wasted an entire sermon on me and my ignorance. I was so heartbroken and so very condemned. He blamed me right there in front of everyone. I felt naked and belittled. It felt like the pastor stripped me down and then let everyone see me in my shame. What if someone had been standing nearby and overheard our conversation prior to his sermon? I was so afraid everyone knew who he was talking about as he broadcasted my deplorable attempt to be obedient to God. The congregation surely must have been even more disappointed than the pastor was.

The fact was, to me, we were a cult. He didn't want us to say those things to people, but it was looked down upon if you didn't look or act a certain way. He called us a "peculiar people." We were not. Personally, I thought we were just plain rude, condemning, modern day pharisees. There were a few true blue and honest people who wanted to seek God. They desired him, but in that kind of environment of condemnation and critique, no one ever runs away excited like the Samaritan woman or the woman caught in adultery. You walk away with your tail tucked between your legs. Or in my case, somewhere hidden under my long, dismal skirt.

We stayed at that church for several years because we started to love the people like family. However, when a person stays in that kind of environment, they become like the environment. The only time Jesus ever scolded anyone was when he spoke with a Pharisee. He sent the sinners away with hope and care. He let them know they were loved in spite of themselves. That's what I wanted to be like toward others, but the longer I stayed in condemnation, the more I condemned others.

I was awful toward my husband. I was never concerned about his porn addiction. I was only concerned about how it was going to affect me and my children. I never thought of Adam. He would lay on the floor and pray because, like he once told me, he couldn't get any lower. I knew he was guilty, but I was too. I wanted him to hurt like he hurt me. I wanted him to be alone like the times he left me to look for prostitutes. I wanted him to pay for all the times he stayed out late to cheat on me. He wouldn't come home for hours after work. Instead, he stopped at the nearest adult store and spent away his stress. I wanted him to feel unwanted like I felt when he wouldn't look at me for months. He called me "pretty" approximately four times during our marriage. I was punishing him, and I never gave it a second thought. I tried to forgive him. I said I forgave him, but the condemnation was there the whole time. Layers of hate piled up onto the wall of lies and deceit that he built. All the graffiti was clearly there on the wall for everyone to see. Guilt, shame, and records of wrongs were written over and over.

I'll never forget the time Adam called me late one night from work. He had recently been promoted to foreman, and we were starting to get caught up on all our bills. It was three hours passed the time he should have been home when the phone rang. His voice was frazzled, and I knew something was very wrong. I braced myself for his confession. He told me he had been inside on the computer at work when he should have been outside with his men. (He was just like King David! He was home and he should have been at war!) The computer froze on a site he had visited, and it wouldn't shut off. He mentioned it was a matter of time before the office workers would see his guilty pleasures all over the computer screen. He knew he was fired.

That night I held his hand and tried to be like Jesus. I was so sick to my stomach, and I said nothing. Word traveled in our small town, and everyone mocked me. "What a fool I was to stay!" the people chattered. I was embarrassed and afraid, but I begged him to spill it all. If there were any more secrets, I needed to know. I didn't think I could live through one more lie. And Adam did just that. He unloaded all the lies and the sick, twisted things he'd done. He even mentioned how he climbed through the attic to see my friends and family use our bathroom during their visits. He proceeded to tell me he'd even watched me shower, and I wasn't the only one he had watched in the shower. There were others that had stayed in our home. This was a sickness far deeper than I could ever imagine. He showed me all the stashes where he hid his cards and books. He told me about the porn sites and the phone calls he made to the eight hundred numbers.

I wasn't enough for him. No one could ever fill his hunger or satisfaction. His appetite was much too great. I was moving beyond the point of numbness, and I couldn't stop it. I should have known, and I let it go too long. There were so many signs.

Church people told me that with God things were easier. I was confused. How was any of this easier? I really thought that I was going to be protected and that boys turn into men with Jesus. I used to tell people that Jesus was my insurance policy, but this religion and all its laws were looking more like a death certificate. My heart was getting harder, my boys were getting older, and this veil of torture that separated me from God was getting thicker. I didn't think God would allow things to get worse, but I was wrong. I was wrong about so much in my life. I was wrong about love, I was wrong about dying at twenty-three, and I was wrong about God.

While I was on a trip to a theme park with my boys, I received a call from my mother about a few medical tests that my stepdad Bill had undergone because of muscle spasms and twitches along with muscle weakness. My mother told me Bill had ALS (Amyotrophic Lateral Sclerosis). There was no cure.

Bill, barely fifty, was going to die. The only man that loved me

Alec's first day of preschool in August 1999. He was four years old. Airic, age two, wanted a picture with his big brother.

Above: Our family trip to the theme park. This was taken right before I received the phone call about my stepdad's diagnosis. Left: My stepdad sitting outside before a breathing treatment in January 2005. By October 2005, he would not be able to breathe on his own and would need a tracheotomy.

was going to leave me alone here in this world. My boys loved him so much, and I didn't know how I could tell them. How could they accept Bill's diagnosis?

I was angry. I was angry at God for giving me this unwelcomed life, and I demanded answers. I never asked for any of this, and I wanted to know what kind of choices I was given.

So many thoughts went through my head with one phone call. The first thought was how could my mother call me here and now with my children? How could I keep it together for another day without them knowing? I thought my mother could have waited one more day until we came home. Our trip was ruined.

Her waiting would never have mattered though. I just didn't want to know at all. It felt better not knowing. Those twenty-four hours with my boys were some of the most difficult. I had to smile and have fun with them while I was tormented inside knowing they'd lose a grandfather and I'd lose the only man that ever truly loved me up to this point.

As tormented as I was, all I knew was I wanted to experience life before death came for me, too, and I wanted out of my marriage. I planned to say my final goodbyes—goodbye to my husband, goodbye to my stepfather, and one big goodbye to me.

5

My Frankenstein

Dear God,

I need help. I need you so badly and I'm so angry with you. You know the heart of all men, so I might as well say it. I'm leaving my husband, and I am moving in with my mom and dad. He needs to be given shots twice a day, and Mom wants me to do it. This is my out, and I'm taking it. It's been nine years of hell, and that's a long time to be unloved. It's a long time to be alone. I just don't want to hurt anymore. Alec and Airic are ten and eight now. There is still time to undo this mess. I'm shielding them from this man who refuses to grow up and be who I need him to be. I can't do this anymore. The people from the church haven't tried to help me, and I don't care anymore. You haven't helped me. How can you, the God of all, be so quiet when I need you most? It is just like that day in my room, pounding on the floor. My dad is going to die if you don't help him. My world is about to get unbearable, and as much as you've helped me in times before, I think I'll ride this one out alone. I'm sorry but I can't follow these rules anymore and see nothing change. I remember the day I said to myself that serving you was my marital insurance. I was so certain, but it got worse. I begged you that no matter what, don't ever let me fall. I fell! You let me go. I'm sick of feeling ugly. I hate the person I've become. I know I shouldn't be ashamed of what I look like, but I am! I quit! Maybe he wouldn't have treated me this way if I were pretty. I want to die. I want to jerk the wheel when I'm in the car. My babies deserve better than all of this. I regret having children with him. I do not regret my kids, but I most certainly regret that man-child. My God, are you trying to kill me? Just do it!

I was furious with God. I wanted to give up. I didn't see the point of serving God if there was no joy. Why should I keep trying to invest and pour into people when I was completely empty? How could I continue this way? I felt like I was lying to everyone, especially God. All I ever heard at church was "Obey! Be good! Stop sinning!" That's all I knew. I was a slave to God, and I felt forced to be happy.

It never made much sense to me that God was so loving, yet a slave driver. No one had told me there was a difference between a slave and a bond servant, let alone a daughter. One is bound by law and forced to work; the other volunteers. Bond servants volunteer their work for the master they serve because they love him. When Jesus died for us, he took us from serving in the outer courts to living in his house with the Father. However, the sermons I heard in church never changed. I was told that I was a humble servant, and that is all I would ever be. I felt forced to work.

I admit I acted like the brother in the story about the prodigal son. So many people read that story and assume that the prodigal son was the only broken person. On the contrary, the angry brother was so enveloped in religion that he missed out on a relationship with his own father. The angry brother never realized that everything his father owned was his all along. He truly believed he had to work in the fields like his father's servants in order to earn favor that he already had. The angry brother should have never been in that field when he heard the party happening to celebrate his prodigal brother's homecoming. He should have been happy his lost brother was alive and well, but instead he was so filled with earning and deserving that he lost out on not only the party, but also the understanding that his brother was not only forgiven and brought back into the family, but alive.

Like the angry brother, we get caught up in making sure we are "good enough" and "working hard enough" to be allowed in the house. We serve all day and night, and we fail to see that we actually already own everything our Father owns. Like the prodigal son, we leave the house and spend everything the Father gave us. We think there is nothing left, and many times we won't even return home to ask. (That's where we get the term "backslider.")

God is a gentle Father, and I know that he is not a rapist, forcing himself on us. Yes, he is rage with our enemies, but he is a safe place for his children. It is much like a lioness lying next to a lion. Is he safe to be around? Absolutely not! She trusts him, though. The lioness knows very well what the lion is capable of, but she knows he is there to protect her and not bring her harm. I didn't feel this type of a healthy relationship with God. I knew He was all power, but I didn't know He was all love, too. We need to know and desire both.

I knew about God but realized that I had no idea who he really was. I felt betrayed, and I just couldn't forgive this mean and scary God I learned about in Sunday school. I even feared that if I prayed for something specific, he may treat my prayer like the monkey's paw. For example, if I prayed for money that we needed or even wanted, I was so afraid that God would answer me in an atrocious manner. Maybe someone would have to die, so I would inherit the money. Or maybe I'd be in a car accident and become injured, so God could pay me through a lawsuit. I'd be crippled from the accident, but I'd surely have my money then. I was terrified of what God would take from me because I thought I had to give something to get something. And that, my friend, is exactly what the law and religion indirectly teach. You scratch my back, and I'll scratch yours. God never asked us to die. He did it of his own free will, and he did it so we wouldn't have to. He is not a monkey's paw, but my great fear caused me to never want to ask God for anything.

❊

Immediately after my mother called with Bill's diagnosis, I moved in with my parents. Moving in with them gave me the perfect way to leave Adam, my husband.

It was so strange to drive down that old back road the day I left, looking in the rearview mirror at my soon-to-be ex-husband. It was exactly like I had told him it would be. Years prior to that day, I had warned him that if he didn't stop, I'd one day put the boys in the backseat and leave him to wave goodbye at them through the back window. It happened. Only this time, I wasn't crying; I had a glacial look on my face. The hatred I had held in all those years spoke louder than words. I wanted to leave, and part of me was ecstatic that everything was happening exactly as I said it would. I'm still not sure if my elation was because I was teaching him that I meant what I said or because I was finally free. What I didn't realize then was the prison was inside of me and I was running from an imaginary freedom.

I had told Adam I only needed space, but a divorce would help clear my head more. I managed to make Adam believe that we shared the same lawyer and that he wanted to help us. The lawyer was not representing Adam, but I knew I had to make him feel as if the lawyer was looking out for the best interest of both of us. Plus, I wanted Adam to pay for the lawyer, and the only way to get him to pay was to lie. Adam believed me, and we decided on everything so perfectly during the dissolution that the judge literally told us he'd never seen such a pleasant divorce. I couldn't have agreed more with him.

I lied my way through the entire dissolution because I planned to do whatever it took to rid myself of Adam and make him pay. Besides telling him we shared the same lawyer and gaining his trust, I told him I still cared, and I didn't. His face was a different kind of blanched white the day I told him the truth. He couldn't believe that I was capable of lies, let alone, lies of that nature. It was unheard of for me to lie, and he knew I learned it all from him. When you study a person long enough, you learn their ways. I can see how Satan knows everything about us. I had learned how to be a perfectly innocent-looking con artist. Add that to being a young female, and you got yourself a very dangerous woman. The look of lethal looked good on me.

During all this great derailing by the devil, I lost my job. My company was sold, and I was on my own with nothing. I knew the grass wasn't greener when I set out on a mission to find a man to financially help me, but I was so lonely. I wanted to be married, just not to Adam.

I spent a lot of time in the bar, and the first man I dated was a straight-up real cowboy. He had the horse, boots, a belt buckle the size of a dinner plate, and all. He was easy on the eyes and a rebel. He was just what I thought I needed. He was great for a matter of two weeks before he started calling me names and throwing me around. I swore I would never be treated that way, and I began to swing back. I'd be lying if I said I didn't like tossing him around a little. I was a gaunt, little thing, but I was stronger than that thick-witted cowboy realized. He didn't know that I wrangled a man twice his size a few times in the arena of woman beaters. Not to mention the fist fights with so many others, including all the boys in my family. They were stepping-stones in all the training I needed. My point is this: I knew how to string a squirrelly man up in seconds flat.

Needless to say, the cowboy broke my heart for a quick second. I saw he liked me, but I heard I was stupid. He took me out on dates at the bar, but I heard I was so pathetic. He called me a bar fly, and I had no idea what that even was. I begged him to just be friends with me, so that I could cope with my father's illness and help my children through the breakup with their father. He insisted we date. I agreed to his ludicrous idea and dated for just a few months. That was my first mistake. Hanging around for those horrible few months was the second. He had been cheating on me with five other women. We all found out about each other, and my heart broke.

I pulled up my bootstraps and decided to date another man. I wanted to make the cowboy jealous. You see, there was a reason for my decision to call up this new man. The cowboy loathed him. At the beginning of when I had started dating the cowboy, this new boyfriend of mine grabbed me inappropriately one night in a bar. He made it obvious and couldn't care less that the cowboy saw what he'd done. The cowboy absolutely hated him for that display of disrespect.

Revenge was mine for the taking, and I knew I could make one phone call and this man would be at my house in less time than you could say "Cowgirl's revenge"! Besides, I knew this man from high school, and I swore to never date a man I didn't know ever again. That was too dangerous with small children. Of course, I made the call, and just like I said, within an hour he was knocking at my door. This man was very large. He wasn't a scrawny little boy anymore. He was full of muscle and now towered over me. He was a two-hundred-and-sixty-pound, six-foot three-inch guy that could take care of me.

That relationship lasted six months—three months of fun and three months of hell. I was unaware that he was an alcoholic and had a temper. One evening we had a party at our home, and friends and family members told me to go wake him up after he had gone to bed early. He became angry at me, and we all thought it was just in fun, but the Goliath was not amused. The evening died down, and I decided to join him in bed. In his eyes, that was a bad idea. In the middle of the night, I woke up to him towering over top of me. His giant hand covered my mouth as his long, thick finger rammed down my throat. I gagged and tried to understand what was happening.

"If I can't sleep, neither can you," he screamed. "How do you like it?"

He finally released his tight grip on my head, and I rolled over. During the time that I was trying to muster the air back into my lungs, he managed to tuck his legs up enough to reach the middle of my back. Then as hard as he could, he kicked me and sent me sailing in mid-air several feet across the room. My body slammed into the wall, and I fell to the floor. When I turned my head to look at him, his eyes were different. He looked like my father that night. I knew he was out of his mind with anger.

My youngest sister Melissa started beating on the locked bedroom door. All she could hear were screams and loud bangs coming from the room. I managed to get up, run to the door, and unlock it. I ran out into the living room where Melissa had been sleeping. I was irate.

I saw his shadow coming down the trailer hallway. I picked up a very large cooler full of water, ice, and beer with my left hand. I then launched it across the room with the palm of my hand. It sailed all the way across the living room, landing right in front of where he was standing. I missed him, and instead it made a loud crash as it landed on my beautiful glass coffee table.

I now had his attention, but I wasn't finished. I walked over to a nearby mirror on the wall and punched it as hard as I could. I just wanted to see blood, even if it was my own. I wanted to feel pain, but I couldn't. I felt nothing in my time of madness.

The room was deadened with silence. There I was, bleeding all over the place. My sister stood there scared to death to move. The colossal human stood staring at me as if I'd lost every bit of sense

I had. I'm certain I had. I looked at my sister, and then I looked at him. I said nothing as I bent down and started cleaning up the large shards of glass. I had blood running down the dangling flesh hanging from what looked like a hand. What did I get myself into and why was it getting worse? No one spoke of that night ever again.

Those were the kind of nights I had with him when we were drinking together. Thankfully, my boys never saw him hit me. On the last night that I was his punching bag, we had yet another fight. He was banging a skillet into his head, and I begged him to stop, but he wouldn't. He threw the skillet on the floor, and nothing but a pile of dented metal remained. He then proceeded to rip up the last twenty dollars I had. I had been planning to buy Alec a pair of pants with that money. I was just done.

I ran outside with a busted lip and a bruised collarbone from where he backhanded me and shook me like a rag doll by my shirt. I called the police to come pick me up. I knew if I called, I'd go. He chased me down the road, and I jumped into a pile of high grass along the side of the road.

The police came. I was in hysterics while he stood there calm and confident. My pain washed all the makeup away as I talked to the policeman. I told him that he had hit me and all the other things that happened. I admitted to backhanding him after he hit and shook me.

The police officer looked me dead in the eyes and said, "Since you hit him, we will take you to jail too, should you decide to press charges."

I begged the police officer to examine my boyfriend for marks. I showed him mine. They were obvious. My lip was enormous, and

I had huge bruises all over my collarbone with a ripped shirt to prove he wasn't innocent. Plus, he had a history of abusing his sister and had even thrown her down the stairs.

I realized at that point no one would ever protect me. I didn't press charges because my boys didn't need a mother with a record. How could the law do that to me?!? Now I couldn't even trust the police.

An officer drove me to my mother's house. Before I cried myself to sleep, my mother took pictures of my beat-up face. I had hopes of awakening the next morning to no proof of what happened to me the night before. My boys would be home soon from the weekend at their father's, and I didn't want them to see how weak I was. I just wanted to forget it all.

I now had no job, no money, no home, and no car. Yes, even my car was unfixable. I was in a perfect position for God to help me, but he still didn't. I stayed at my mother's for a few days before going to my ex-father-in-law's house. I called my ex-husband to come get me.

I told Adam that we could date each other again, but I wanted to be an exotic dancer. Both of us thought it was the perfect idea. I couldn't criticize Adam for his addictions, and he couldn't belittle me for becoming the very thing he lusted after. Not to mention, exotic women were the beautiful poison that tore us apart.

I started my ruinous occupation in October, and the clientele welcomed me with open arms. I was still young enough to dance, and the hunger for more attention became addictive. The men had an appetite for me, and the feeling was mutual. My desire was to allow each individual to see me as they needed to see me. I would become all of their worthless hopes and made-up dreams. I'd be their everything.

I quickly became very famous in that small town. They called me Barbie—branded and beautiful, ready to take the stage. I hated that name with all my being because as I grew into a young adult, my hair was bleached blonde and grew past my waist. It was beautiful. I had an hourglass figure, and the longest legs you'd ever seen. I always thought of myself as the ugly duckling. Once I grew out of the awkward stages of my youth, I was much more attractive. People would refer to me as Barbie. Some said I looked fake along with other snide remarks. Others meant it as a compliment. On top of that, Grammy always called me her little Barbie Girl. I just wanted a new name, but I guess if it brought the people, and the people brought the money, who cared?

My job description was as follows: Be beautiful, be fun, be a con artist, and drink as much as you like. I was a perfect fit. Thanks to Adam, I had learned how to be a con artist. My photo was immediately placed on the business cards and used in the weekly newspaper ads to attract the local or traveling loners. I started traveling with my boss on vacations and became her prize. She hosted me in her home and at many VIP swim parties. She even invited me to celebrate her birthday in Vegas, and I was beside her on holidays. One dancer stated in anger that I was the apple of her eye. This was true. She showed me off, and even to this day, my face remains on the business cards.

At one New Year's Eve party, which my boss had asked me

to spend with her and a few others for the weekend, she told me to ask the DJ to play a song I'd never heard before. She then gave me a fedora and said, "Keep it classy, Barbie Doll, and take your place on the dance floor."

So many people were dancing and celebrating the New Year on the dance floor that anyone else would've shied away, but I was hardly shy. I loved to dance. I loved to lose myself in the song. The song was my beloved, and dancing was my expression of devotion.

Me on the gentleman's club business card. They are still being printed to this day.

The song began, and it was evident that it was a striptease genre. I did what my boss asked of me, and I was instantly lost in the song. As the song ended, I heard clapping and cheering. I was a little confused as I stood there and saw an enormous circle around me made up of every single person in that beautiful place. I walked back over to where my boss was sitting surrounded by people begging to know my name. My boss kept shouting where I was located, and it sounded like I was being auctioned off. Men and women alike stood there waiting to see where they could get more of what I had just done. My boss knew what she was doing. I smiled and watched her. She looked up at me and said, "It's just business, baby."

I smiled and thought, "Not one stitch of clothing was removed." I laughed to myself with a pride-filled snicker. "Man, I am just that good."

I became the figment of both male and female imaginations. I was a shadow of what they wanted or wanted to be. I craved the attention and enjoyed every second of it. I went from a poor little broken nothing to this woman that paid for nothing anywhere she went. Men from all over the world demanded my presence. Owners from other strip clubs would come to see the blonde bombshell. It thrilled me to leave them speechless. Men would laugh at the rich bar owners because of their lack of composure at my very presence. This power I had over men became my superpower, and I now was lethal. I was Barbie. And that's all they'd ever get close enough to know about me.

I don't say these things to make anyone think I was big-headed. Actually, I was quite the opposite. I was a lonely shell, and you couldn't have found a pulse if you tried to. I died inside with every dance, shower show, and champagne bottle. I was enough for every man in that bar, but I wasn't enough for myself. Part of me wanted it that way so that I couldn't get hurt again. I hated men for hurting me; I hated women for hating me.

There is a sadness that dwells in the hand-me-down heart of a stripper. The black light hid the scars of my heart and only reflected the glitter. The aroma of pain and the scent of cotton candy filled the nostrils of the eager men. The secret was to wear enough cotton candy to mask the pain.

I had become a professional con. The money was easy, and I was always invited into the imagination of my devoted suitors. I was a sexy devil shark, and I loved the power I had to make a man melt at the very idea of being with me. I'd tell some men I wanted to write a book and finish school. I'd tell others I wanted to travel the world. Some men longed to hear me say I only wanted to settle down and be a good wife. It all depended on the first two minutes of our conversation, and I knew what they wanted to hear.

I used to laugh and ask women all the time why a man would give up so much for a dancer in the dark. Men would pay hundreds of dollars for an evening with me on a black leather couch. Talk was not so cheap. I had heard about a man remortgaging his home for me. Another man spent twenty thousand dollars on a vacation I took with my boss. I kept the reality of lying for money tucked away in my mind. I deadened any awareness I could to stay focused on the task at hand. I had never wanted to live in this morbid reality, so I drowned it all out with a Jager Bomb and a good song. I can remember only a few times, in a drunken stupor, crying to a co-worker of how awful I was to take so much from these people. My pain would last until six o'clock in the evening when I took a shot and entered the spotlight. Guilt tastes fine with a shot of whiskey and shame.

I said I would only dance for a few months in order to get my car fixed and until I found a job. However, I found myself not able to leave because the money was so good. I made a lot in that tiny bar. During a slow month, working a mere twenty hours, I brought home close to ten thousand dollars a month. That wasn't counting all the clothes, booze, drugs, parties, and vacation spots. It may have been a small town, but I was not afraid to own it. I needed the atmosphere more than anything. Why would any woman leave? Let me rephrase that: Why would any heartbroken woman leave?

I'll never forget the October I started there. In just the first few weeks of working, I met so many people. I met famous people and the bodyguards of famous people. Strangely, they treated me like royalty. I too was famous there. I was in complete control, but deep down that control meant nothing to me. I was empty. The truth of the matter was everything was all smoke and mirrors. None of it was glamorous. Makeup and black lights hid it all.

People would ask me how I could do what I did. Some people asked out of sheer curiosity, and others asked in a demeaning manner. My answer was always the same: You can go numb in any job. It's the same as the rest. You get used to it.

One day, a regular client came in with someone I'd never seen before. I strolled up to this enormous, statuesque man and asked who he was. His eyes were alluring, and I'd never seen a man so perfectly masculine in all my days. He was a man so insanely beautiful that he stopped me in my tracks. That had never happened before in my life. No man ever made me look twice, let alone lose a breath. It was evident that he was using steroids, but I didn't care. His distended biceps looked as if they were trying to escape his tight-fitting shirt. I couldn't help but notice his rippling pectorals were perfectly placed on his muscular, tanned body. I could stare at him for all eternity and never grow weary. This one could definitely be the lullaby to quiet my nightmare.

Tommy Miller around the time I met him in October 2006

I didn't care where he came from or why he was there at that moment. I wanted to own him. I wanted him to own only me. I wanted to know more about him. More importantly, I wanted him to know me. Oh, but isn't that the game, anyways? It's all a game.

I approached him with the normal man/stripper lingo, but this time, I really wanted to know his name—Tommy. I scolded the regular client who brought this man-feast to my table. I told him he should have never brought Tommy because it would make my job very difficult. I was intensely serious. No way could I focus with this eye teaser in front of me. The bewitching man quickly hid his hands, and I sat down. I asked him for a drink, and he whispered to his friend. The regular quickly got the bartender's attention.

I didn't know at the time that this perfect picture of what a man is was underage and unable to buy me a drink. I wouldn't know for several more months. He was eighteen and afraid to tell me. He kept his hands hidden under the table at all costs because the enormous X's screamed, "I'm much too young for you." (I was twenty-eight and scared him to death.)

He had to know the commotion he caused when he walked into the bar that first time. He turned the heads of all the dancers and most of the customers. His beauty was impeccable, and he knew it, too. He was sweet, yet cocky, and I liked it.

He made me nervous, but I never let him know it. Whenever he visited me, I would walk up to him perfectly and walk away even more perfectly when I left him. That was the most important part to remember—it was always in the walk-away.

One year and two months went by, and Tommy decided to ask me to have coffee. We had become great friends and shared our ideas and thoughts along with information about our love lives. I had imagined many times that it was me in place of his girlfriends. I never let on that I was falling in love with him. I wanted so much more from him, but I knew he didn't see me the same way. What man shares secrets about his women with a woman he is attracted to? If I couldn't have him, I'd settle for what he could give of himself. So, coffee it would be. Going out with someone from the club was a no-no for me, especially during the day, but I couldn't refuse him.

I may have worked in a strip club, but the owner was amazing! When I mentioned Tommy to her, she gave me a cocky grin. "Be careful, Barbie Girl. He is a hot one and you could fall for him." She knew my weakness for this one and wasn't afraid to offer me a word of caution. I loved her dearly. She may have owned a club that defiled all of God's ideas of man and woman, but she was loved greatly by all the girls because she always gave her heart. She loved us and we loved her.

Despite her business advice, Mr. Gorgeous and I decided to date. We thought maybe this relationship thing, even with our age difference, could work. He told me later how afraid of me he was. I would have never known he had an interest in me if I hadn't just come out and blatantly showed interest in him myself. A little shot of liquid courage goes a long way. After all, he may have been a charmer, but when he talked to me, it was as if all sense left him. There were quite a few occasions when his intellect abandoned him, but one moment in particular comes to mind. We were having coffee at a restaurant when he looked up at me and genuinely said, "I wish I could find someone like you, only younger." I thought all chances were out the door that day. All I could do was laugh and state that his love could be right in front of him. To this day, I still remind him of his brainless remark; just for fun, of course. We laugh about it from time to time, and it takes me back to the flirty love games we played. Frankly, it was quite tortuous playing with the idea of not knowing what we would become, or better yet, not become.

6

The Chrysalis

Dear God,

I'm not interested in a bound relationship with you. Time after time they haven't done me a lot of good. I am quite interested in how this will all turn out, though. I'm so sick and so tired of just surviving. I remember sitting in my church years ago beside my ex-husband wondering if this was all there was. Not so much the life with him and my sons, but regarding you. Do you remember? Of course, you do. Nothing gets past you. I'm to the point I haven't the slightest clue who I am. What's worse is who am I even supposed to be? What could I be? Look at me. Really look at me, God! I'm a used-up woman. How did I let this happen? Better yet, how did you let this happen to me? You know I begged you not to let me fall. Well, well. Isn't this just a pretty sight? I hope you like it. You'll be looking at this for a while. So, what's the catch? What's with the new guy? Please keep the element of surprise out of this. I'm over that, too. Amen.

A disturbing fear filled the air. The smell of winter and past relationships chilled my bones. Fall was ending soon, and the smell of bonfires interlaced with the bitter blast of arctic breaths flowed through the trees, now stripped of their beautiful foliage. I cringed. I hated this time of year. The time when everything warm and beautiful seems to die. I had given up hope that everything I'd ever wanted was going to happen, so I guess I decided to add a few more outlandish memories to my collection and have another dance with the devil.

While I was adjusting to a new relationship, my stepdad Bill was bedridden and very ill. I had moved back in with my mom and dad to get out of my ex's way and start life over…yet again. I stopped drinking and started going to the gym with my new beau, Tommy, who was a model and a competitive bodybuilder. We couldn't go anywhere together without the world staring at us. If it wasn't me they were looking at, it was him. I wasn't used to sharing attention, and truthfully, neither was he. He told me once that in past relationships, as he hugged his girlfriends, he was always looking over their shoulder to see if there was anything better. I thought that was extremely arrogant until I realized I had done the same thing my whole life.

Working at the bar became harder and harder. I was sober and hated the atmosphere. I couldn't lie as well or play the con game as clever as before. I was falling out of love with the song and just couldn't lose myself anymore. I wanted to, but the desire was overtaken by a new drug—love. The money started to slow down, and the only thing that increased was the pain I caused myself and others. The regret also deepened by the day. I couldn't look a man or woman in the eyes without seeing Tommy. The worthlessness and despair ate me alive, causing me to want to get wasted, but

I couldn't because Tommy had asked me not to drink anymore while at work.

I didn't realize, throughout our year of friendship, all the things Tommy had seen me do, all the lies I told to others, and all the idiotic moments I had while intoxicated. He began to question all the things I said to him. He wondered if they were cold-hearted lies, too. A stripper never intends to take you home for more than just a hookup. God forbid, she shares her personal life with you, either. I knew too much about him, and he knew way too much about me. I told him I wanted to quit work, and he took this as things between us were getting serious. I wanted him to see I wasn't just another one of his bobble-headed college girls. I was a woman, and I was fully grown.

One evening we were driving to my mom and dad's place, and Tommy was acting so strangely. I started to cry as I truly believed he was going to leave me that night. He spoke with my mother and stepfather alone before telling me to come back to the room where Bill lay in his bed. Tommy, in tears, sat me down, got on bended knee, and proposed.

I was ecstatic! This man was in my stepfather's room asking for my hand in marriage. Some girls dream of elaborate proposals with candlelight and flowers, but to me, Tommy's choice to propose in front of Bill and my mother was perfect. I wanted Bill to be proud of me. To see the twinkle of approval in his eyes was the most beautiful thing. Tommy had found a way to make sure Bill was a part of our decision, and that is a memory forever burned into my heart. My mind took a picture that day and locked it away, a special moment forever mine to keep.

Tommy honored me that day by asking Bill for my hand in marriage, and he showed respect for the man that laid in that bed. He wanted to make sure Bill knew he had a choice to give his blessing for our marriage or not. Because Bill's deteriorating condition left him with only eye movement, Tommy was unsure of how he could ask Bill. So he spoke with my mother to learn how to communicate. She told Tommy that Bill would respond with his eyes, and she instructed him on how to talk to Bill. She also said she would be in the room to help decipher if necessary.

Tommy told me that when he entered Bill's room, he said to Bill, "I want to marry your daughter. I love her very much and want to take care of her and her boys. If that's okay, look right at the wall. If not, look left at the wall."

Bill looked to the right. I asked Tommy what he thought when my stepdad said yes. I wanted to know what happened in the room because I would have loved to have seen that precious moment between Tommy and Bill. Tommy told me that when Bill said yes, lots of thoughts raced through his mind.

I looked at him a little shocked. I thought he was going to tell me that he was excited, but he didn't say that. He told me at that moment in time, he didn't truly understand Bill's disease. He didn't know that ALS may cause a person to be unable to move any muscle in their body, but their mind remains completely coherent. He told me that he thought to himself, "What choice does Bill have? How could he approve? He barely knows me." After seeing Bill's eyes shift to the right, he had one final thought that reassured him. He knew Bill trusted me. He knew I loved my stepdad with all my heart and soul and respected his wishes. Bill wanted me, Alec, and Airic to be happy. It was evident that he approved of Tommy. It was time to propose.

I was more than ready to give up dancing at this point in my life. I couldn't bear the thought of losing this man. I was sober, in the best physical shape of my life, and ready for my turn at the dinner table of love—until I thought about the bills rolling in. Having money does strange things to people. I owned a lot of things that I didn't need. I had made a few purchases, and a brand new four-wheeler was one I hadn't finished paying off. How could I quit? Where would I go to make this money? I was in a trap, and I needed out.

Besides, who buys a dance from a girl wearing an enormous rock? I'll tell you—no one! People started telling me to take the ring off while I was working and not to talk about him so much. After all, I was the queen of con. I found myself unable to. They told me to leave him because we moved too fast. (We started dating at the end of November, and we were engaged by January 10.) I was amazed that so many people had the greatest advice to give, and not one of them could have cared less prior to the engagement. People were coming out of the woodwork proclaiming their love for me. I'm sure they all feared the thought that any chances of being with me would be over.

My ex-husband even told me to seriously think of what I could ever give Tommy. "You could give him nothing. No children and no future." Those were my ex-husband's words, and I started to believe him. I could no longer have children. So, I tried to leave my relationship with Tommy.

I was so heartbroken. I didn't want this perfect being to have a used-up, trashy woman pulling him down. He was in school working toward his degree. He had a future, and I thought it wasn't with me. While I hoped Tommy would refuse to let me go, I had never before had a man fight for me.

Much to my surprise, Tommy wasn't having it. He refused to let me leave him. He saw things differently and embraced me with tears in his eyes. He begged me not to leave. I could feel the sincerity and desperation crying out. I didn't know how to handle that response.

He loved me on purpose.

He loved me right where I was in my life—a broken, depressed, mother of two with a past that could scare away the devil himself.

He loved me like my stepfather loved me.

He loved my boys.

He loved my family, and I just couldn't let that go no matter how selfish I was being.

We planned to wait for four years so that Tommy could graduate from college before we married, but God had other plans.

Bill was getting worse by the day. He was completely reliant on my mother. He couldn't shut his eyes, so she'd close them for him. My mother was stricken with such fear of losing him that she topped the generator off with gas every morning in case the power went out. She tried to keep him even if it was just a beautiful spirit trapped in a man of stone. She was broken physically and drained mentally.

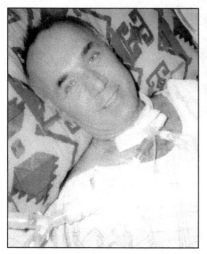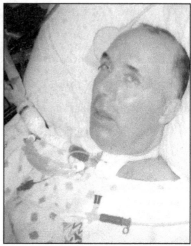

Left: Bill could still smile after his tracheotomy in October 2005. Right: In February 2006, four short months after the tracheotomy, Bill had a feeding tube and could no longer move anything except his eyes.

The disease was just too much on Bill. He no longer looked like my father. All of his muscle tone had changed its shape. His face drooped along with his withered, weakened body. The strong hands he once had were shapeless. His eyes, though, oh, his eyes could still speak words of care and love in a thousand ways. Those eyes told us he would always love us.

Then that dreaded day came. I got the call that my mother had to let Bill go. We gathered the family together and waited with him in his hospital room. We held his hand and whispered how much we loved him. We kissed his forehead, and I stepped back for the others to express their heartfelt goodbyes. The nurse stood on the right side of the bed checking his vitals, and we stared at his chest rising and falling. We watched so quietly in fear of missing anything.

The nurse looked up and said, "He's gone."

I thought I was ready and had already determined that I would be the rock for my mother and sisters. But I couldn't breathe. I couldn't take it. I started to hyperventilate, and I passed out on the hospital floor. My daddy was sleeping and would never wake up.

My father, because he truly was a father to me in every way except birth, passed away on April 20, 2007. I kept hearing his voice over and over—the last words he said before they did the tracheotomy. It was raspy and weak, but the words "I love you" will always play in my ears when I need him the most, like a song stuck inside your mind playing over and over. "I love you" was all I needed to hold on.

It's so amazing how we remember our loved ones. Bill never knew this, but I studied him. I stared and watched his every move while he became sicker. I took pictures with my mind and locked them away for only me to see. I can still see the way he held a cheeseburger and the way he folded his hands at the table. Those are the things I see when I close my eyes and think of him.

My mom was as steady as a rock. She was our sure support and foundation. She was so hurt, but I knew she was exhausted and needed Bill to rest. She couldn't watch him suffer anymore. My dad had a sister that was always there for my mom and my dad. She cared deeply for my father and helped my mother with true care and consideration. She may never know how much I appreciated her and her twin boys. There aren't words to describe the sacrifices she made coming from another state to be with them. For that, surely they will all be blessed. One sister came, but it was exactly all they needed.

Now, it was done. My father was sleeping, and it was time to

December 2004—My stepdad Bill and I hanging out together at the house I had rented after my divorce.

fellowship with the friends and family that showered us with love. We waited four days before putting his body to rest. Everything had been taken care of because my father picked out his casket and clothing before he lost the ability to walk.

On April 24, 2007, we laid my father in the ground where only his temporary body would remain. I knew he was with the Lord. I knew he was safe. I wasn't, though. I was heartbroken beyond what I could bear. My children were devastated, and I didn't even know where to begin to help them. My mom's world was forever changed. My little sisters' worlds were forever changed. I was forever changed.

The day we buried Bill, a memory flooded back into my mind. After we returned home from the theme park, I was sitting in a chair in the backyard thinking about Bill and crying quietly. Adam walked out to see me, and I will never forget the words that he said to me: "Why don't you just get over it?" I was utterly undone. He had lost his mother when I was seven months pregnant with our oldest son, Alec. It had been a hard time for my ex-husband. But I don't recall seeing him cry, at least he never let me see him. (Crying is a weakness in a man is what I was often told.) Perhaps he was able to "get over it," but I wasn't. Maybe he didn't want to hurt or see me hurt anymore. I'm unsure, but his callousness only hardened my already impenetrable heart. My heart was dead, and all I said to him was "What have you done?"

As we sat and ate with family on the afternoon of Bill's funeral, I leaned over to Tommy and said, "Dad would not have wanted us to remember this day like this."

With wide eyes, Tommy said, "Marry me."

"I already said yes."

"No. Today! Now!"

I was ecstatic because that was what my happy, bubbly dad would have wanted. I walked up to my mother, whispered to her, and asked if she thought he would have wanted us to get married that day. Her face smiled with a very accepting "yes"! I saw my dad's happiness all over her.

Next, I asked Alec and Airic what they thought. They were so excited and were ready to go out the door immediately. We called the courthouse, and our family of four headed out.

On the balcony of a courthouse on the saddest day of my life, I felt renewed. Tommy, Alec, and Airic were all I needed at that point. I felt like something good came from the depths of my agony. But I knew I'd never get over my father's death. Never! I know now that I didn't have to. I have a family to help me get through it.

Some of my family were not impressed, and in fact, were quite angry that we chose to get married that day. At first, they said it was disrespectful and that I was trying to pull all the attention on myself. I could only think to myself, "My God, yes! Someone please distract me!" However, this was not the case. We weren't being disrespectful or seeking attention.

It wasn't until the first anniversary of my father's death that their anger released and their eyes opened to the purpose of why we did what we did. I couldn't believe that a year had passed by. They all called me with such happiness in their voices. They told me that, instead of waking up with the pain of remembering the sadness, they thought of us creating a life together. My heart was overwhelmed, and I thought about how Bill would have wanted it that way.

So, we started our new life together as a new family. There were quite a few bugs we needed to work out. Let's just say, there was a little Frankenstein in the unhealed and, might I add, very hidden parts of my heart. This monster had established residence in my mind before I could remember. It would take a long process of prayers and changing my thoughts daily to kill this monster. The battle in my mind was just beginning.

7

Cheers!

God,

Is this my break? How can I have hope so desperate, yet feel as if I'm standing on the edge of the imaginary cliff of my future? If I hope in you, I can drop and free fall with ease. Unfortunately, I am fully tense and waiting for the edge to crumble beneath my feet once again. I'm exhausted with feeling as if I'm destined to sink the rest of my life in a quicksand leading to hell. The more I move, the more I sink. So, I'll stay still and see how long you give me to breathe. Do me a favor and at least care enough for my boys. I've run them through enough muck with my so-called "plans of a better life." They need a father. They need steadiness. Me—who cares? Just help them. Amen.

Tommy and I started our marriage with nothing. When I left my ex-husband, I didn't take anything but my clothes and my boys. I left everything behind in that broken home. It didn't seem difficult. I had all I needed in my silver Sunfire, including what dignity I had left.

So, when I quit my job, it created a much larger problem—

bills. Car payments, four-wheeler payments, school clothes. I had absolutely nothing I could contribute financially except more bills. Tommy went on a mission at nineteen years old to get a job that would support a ready-made family of four. I, too, was looking for work. With the reputation I had, I knew being hired somewhere would not be an easy task. After my first marriage ended and before I worked at the strip club, I had worked in a convenience store where I was the "application gatekeeper" for my boss. I knew firsthand the judgment I would be facing.

One day a beautiful young woman had come into the store. She was seeking employment and asked me for an application. I was happy to help her. We needed a few extra hands to pick up the hours we were all trying to juggle. She filled out the application, politely handed it back to me, smiled nervously, and said, "Thank you."

Whenever I took applications, my boss and I used a little trick. If I marked a happy face on an application, that one quickly went to the top of the hiring list. If I put a sad face or any other remarks mimicking the "My God, don't hire" attitude, it either went to the bottom for desperate situations or was simply tossed into the trash. So, as the young woman was exiting the store, I glanced at her application. Near the end of her application, it noted her only job other than fast-food worker was an exotic dancer.

To me, she didn't look like a dancer. She was beautiful and didn't portray any of those insidious characteristics. And she couldn't have been more than twenty years old. No matter though, I was disgusted with the woman. How dare she even think to bring her trash into our store and expect a real honest job! I wrote quite a few mean and negative remarks on her application. I became so angry that I took it to my boss and showed her this vile-excuse-of-a-person's application.

My boss was as disgusted as I was. I told her there was "no way in hell a whore would work with us." I'm sorry to be so blunt, but that was what came out of my mouth. I was not sorry at the time, to say the least. I was angry. But, why?

I look back at that situation, and I cry. I cry often. That woman was so young. Did she have children? What was her story? I was too blinded by the pain and wrong done to me that I couldn't see her need for help. She was everything I hated. She was the reason I was divorced in the first place. My ex-husband longed and sought out women like her. They ruined lives. At least that's what I thought. Oh, the shame I feel when I think of her beautiful face.

I still pray that I will see her again one day. I would hold her and apologize for my actions. I'd hug her and tell her she is perfect. Maybe that is what I searched for as well—someone to just look inside me and see what was really happening.

As I applied for work, so many women judged me. I experienced all that the beautiful young woman felt. I was her. I was the whore hated in my small town. No one cared about my story. They didn't ask how something like this could happen to a good girl with two little boys. They took one look and threw me out like the trash they thought I was.

At this point I wanted Tommy to get me out of our town as fast as possible. We found a tiny house to rent in a nearby town where Tommy had grown up. The new location worked for a while until I started to resent him for taking me out of my hometown. I hated my hometown, yet I was dependent on its familiarity. I had no business staying in that dark, poor excuse for a village, but it was all I knew and I wanted to go back.

Isn't it interesting how well we decorate our prisons? Mine had beautiful frilly curtains and was so very comfy. It's a dangerous thing to decorate the prison you've allowed yourself to enter. Have you ever walked into someone's home and looked around? When you aren't familiar with something, you notice everything. When the elephant in the room lives with you for unending years, it just becomes another knickknack on the shelf. You forget about it and move on about your day. Everyone else can see it sitting there, but you become blind to its familiarity. You are used to its grotesque, oversized accumulation of problems. It takes up space in your life, yet you have no trouble just gently stepping over it. Some people have even gone as far as dressing it up to be part of the family. Familiarity is as dangerous as befriending a wild animal. You may have a wonderful love for it, but never take your eyes from it. It will forever be preparing its supper, and you will be its submissive feast. Keep in mind that your prison may be pleasantly pristine, but it awaits to shut its deadly doors to embrace you in its belly forever.

Tommy and I started having arguments every weekend. I felt trapped. I wanted to have a few drinks every other weekend while the boys spent time with Adam, their father. Tommy hated the idea of me drinking, and it started causing more problems. Not only was I feeling homesick, but I was feeling controlled. Being controlled was one thing I swore would never happen again. The bickering became worse, and I think we talked about divorce every weekend.

I finally forced myself to get a job at a nearby gas station just so I could get to know the townspeople. I thought the job would help me start over. It didn't. I was mocked and not accepted or welcomed by any means at all. I specifically remember a man standing in line, waiting on me to help him, when I caught him taking a picture of me. I saw my face on the front of his camera phone. He took off to the front of the store, and I ran to catch up with him. I thought for sure I'd be fired for chasing down a customer like a wild banshee in pursuit.

I hated that the stranger treated me like a piece of meat. Who was he going to show my picture to? Was he going to keep it for himself? Was he going to blast me over the internet? I hated the way he made me feel. I felt like he took something from me. He took my dignity. What dignity I had left was being stolen once again by another man. I felt worthless. I was nothing but shreds of leftover life. Veiled face, crying bitterly inside, I'd only herald death. I felt nothing good could come from me. I felt like a small woman shrieking deeply from the empty innards I once called a soul. I felt left by God, red-eyed to lament all my days. I wanted to hurt him. I wanted to hurt him the way he hurt me. I wanted to smack him across the face and tell him what I thought of him. Then I pictured my boys. I pictured Tommy. I wondered who else would hire me. I had no choice, and I had to take the disrespect once again. The way that man made me feel inside was low. He treated me like the stripper I had been. I was not for sale. But even if I were for sale, I'd be worthless.

When I caught up with the man and asked him, he denied taking any pictures. I so badly wanted to grab that phone out of his hands and smash it to pieces on the cement floor. I wanted to blare a deafening scream in his face and expose the death I could bring just by my cursed presence. I wanted him to be humiliated like I was, but I just stared at him for what seemed like hours. He knew. I knew. God knew.

Once again, I walked away. This time, with no pride, no posture, and no hope of anything ever changing. I was branded a letter. W was my letter—worthless, waste, and wretched. I felt so defeated. How could I let him mock me? Everyone I looked at looked back at me screaming "Guilty!" with their eyes. I felt like I was living in the story The Tell-Tale Heart. The only difference was I could see the shame and guilt. I heard a small voice in my head say, "Could he just maybe want a picture of you? Maybe he thought you were pretty." No way! Being pretty meant I could be worth something. That thought left my mind as fast as it entered it.

Weeks later, I was approached by a young lady that worked with me. She pulled me aside to tell me our female coworkers felt uncomfortable with me there. I covered my face with my hands, and I cried hysterically. The young lady tried to comfort me, but she couldn't.

I had thought I could start over. But people wouldn't let me forget. I couldn't go anywhere without someone screaming, "Barbie!" I hated that name! Every time my past came up, no matter who brought it up, Tommy became furious for days. I recognized that he held quite a bit of resentment toward me. He wanted my old life to go away. He didn't want people to see me that way. I was his and his alone. They had seen my body uncovered. How could I be special to him when I offered him what everyone else had seen? He wanted them all to forget, too.

No one understood the stress in my mind. I paid the price

heavily. I was fighting everyone, everywhere. Nowhere was safe for me to be myself. I couldn't win. I wanted another chance, and no one wanted to give it to me. I became more and more calloused.

The heart goes through stages. At first, the heart is soft and malleable. Once its soft flesh is pierced over and over, the scars of hurt and devastation cover its formerly unblemished nature. Now, the heart is nothing but disfigured flesh from the trauma. It's hardened for protection so hurt will never lacerate it again. That was the stage my heart was in.

I wanted to forget it all. I wanted to feel like I was lost in the song again. I never wanted to go back there, but I didn't want to feel anything either. I wanted another drink. Drink after drink and weekend after weekend seemed to be the new norm. It seemed as though everyone hated me and I hated me.

So, here's to the girl in the high-heeled shoes, may she take all your money and drink all your booze. Cheers!

8

Where Did You Come From?

God,
What's to say? You don't need to tell me how bad I am. I know enough for the both of us. I'll probably be heading back to the club if this doesn't get fixed soon. Who cares anymore, anyways? I don't.

From the outside looking in, Tommy and I were the perfect couple. We were both attractive. We had the perfect family—two great dogs and the greatest boys in the world. But all those silly fools on the outside looking in couldn't have been more wrong. What else is there to life but to live a wretched life and then die? That's what I believed at this point.

I didn't realize that over the years my youngest son, Airic, had heard all the arguments. I figured he was young and unscathed, but he and his brother sensed how angry I was inside. They just never really knew why.

Airic was also tired of the chaos. We all were. So, when he begged to go to a youth camp our neighbors had invited him to, I let him go. I figured he'd have fun and they wouldn't mess him up too much with bad doctrine. When he returned, we were shocked. We had no clue what had happened to him at camp, but it was drastic. Where was our ornery little redhead? He had definitely been replaced by a kind, caring, young man. He wasn't yelling or fighting with his brother. He was helping me throughout the house and more than willing to go the extra mile with generosity. He was showing kindness where sarcasm used to be, and he was becoming quite the gentleman. I was so proud of his growth from just a week at camp.

Then he insisted that we needed to go to church because he wanted us all to experience what he had experienced. He threatened that if we didn't go to church, he would move in with his biological father. This threat caught our attention because we recognized his desperation.

However, I feared that he had no idea what it was like to attend church and live under the law of God. I didn't want him to grow up to be like those men at the previous churches we had attended. They treated their women as though they were concubines in their own homes. Most of the men dominated their women and lived by the motto "Do as I say, not as I do."

I was afraid to attend church because I honestly didn't want to give up my makeup, jeans, or freedom ever again to such a cruel God. I was also afraid that this church was not like my old church and even more afraid that it was. On the other hand, Tommy immediately agreed to go with Airic, which appeased him for a moment. Tommy was looking for help too.

Tommy came home red-eyed and weepy that first Sunday. I asked what was wrong. He cried with great emotion trying to sputter out how he met God. I was so calloused that I might have even rolled my eyes at the mere idea of him meeting God.

Every Sunday morning, Tommy and Airic trod off to this church where supposedly God was. I was somewhat curious about what was happening to them. They were changing, and no matter how much I tried to pick a fight with Tommy, a fight never surfaced. Tommy was intentionally being very careful with me because he knew if he pushed me, I'd rebel even harder.

I started to get a little jealous over the fact that Tommy and Airic were so happy and how all they talked about was God and the fun they had at church. They were constantly bringing up different church members' names and losing me in the conversation. So, after about a month, I decided to try the whole church thing. In the back of my mind I decided that if they didn't say what I wanted to hear, I'd rip my son out of that church so fast that their heads would spin.

I sat through that first service and stared at the women with their pants and their short hair. I studied every one of them. Several women even went out of their way to talk to me making me feel genuinely cared for. The pastor and his wife were loving and made people feel as if they mattered. They spoke the truth, but not in a way that made me feel bad about myself. Everything the pastor said I had heard before, but this time, it was with a whole new perspective.

How could I not feel bad? Why didn't I feel bad? What was this? Was this God? The real God? Where did he come from?

Where had he been? I was more confused than ever. Yet, a strong thought kept resonating in my mind—What if there is more to this? What if God is nothing like I thought?

For the first time in a long time, I felt something other than shame and self-disgust. To me, feeling anything at all was good. God was whittling away some of the hardest parts of my broken heart and I knew it. I started to feel comfortable with the idea that this life could be so much more.

My experience with going to church and allowing God to heal me reminds me of going to the dentist. You beg for something to numb your mouth, so you won't feel anything. Then as the numbness leaves, you start to feel. Sometimes what you feel doesn't feel good. Pain surfaces and you have to handle it until your problem is healed. With everything that I had been through, I begged God to keep me numb. I didn't want to heal or feel anything ever again. Then I went to church, and the numbness started to wear off.

I felt like I was being set free from so many things. I started to see glimpses of who I used to be before the lies and betrayal of my past. My wounds were healing and turning into scars. I felt the love I had prayed away returning to my heart. My prison was no longer decorated, and I saw it for what it was. Remnants of the past still lingered, but I was definitely moving away from it. I was at fault for keeping myself in my prison of pity. Now I was standing up and walking out of that proverbial confinement and never looking back. This was only the beginning.

My oldest son, Alec, had just turned fifteen and was not on board with going to church. He too had been fed and, might I add, overstuffed with religion. Around the same time Airic went to camp, we noticed strange behaviors from Alec and discovered medications missing from our medicine cabinet. Alec started passing out, and we had no idea why. We searched his room over and over but found nothing. Then Airic confided in me that Alec was cutting himself. He pierced his hips and any skin he was able to run a thick bar through.

After some time passed, Alec came to us in fear. Several people had witnessed things being thrown in his room, and he was now afraid to sleep there. Tommy knew what was happening and told Alec to bring any drugs or paraphernalia to us immediately. Alec went upstairs and brought down several items. He had been huffing gasoline and brought down his homemade rig. He showed us his cuts and the pipe he shoved through his skin. And he told us he'd been practicing witchcraft among other demonic activities.

I stood there, frantic, yet unable to speak. I was looking at my baby's poor little hips with pipes piercing them and cuts everywhere. He wasn't well. When he told us he was having suicidal thoughts, we immediately took him to a doctor, and they admitted him to a psychiatric hospital for three days. They also referred him to a cardiologist who told us Alec had a weak heart due to drug use and he needed heart medication. We also found out that his lungs were burned slightly from the gasoline and other inhalants he had been breathing in. When he came home from the psychiatric hospital, they told us to lock up all knives and anything he could cut himself with. This was so demoralizing to me. He wanted to cut his steak and needed permission. My heart was shattered.

Alec told us that he wanted to stay with his biological father to clear his head. His moving only made things worse, and his behavior went downhill. I told him he needed to come home, but he fought me tooth and nail. He hated me at this point, but I just wanted him safe at home. Tommy, Airic, and I along with the neighbors who had invited Airic to camp decided to take turns fasting every day until Alec came home on his own. We needed a breakthrough.

Two weeks passed, and there was a knock at the door. It was Airic standing there like the prodigal son. He looked as if he wasn't sure we'd accept him. All he could mutter was "I wanna come home." Then he and Tommy embraced each other and wept. I stood there thanking God under my breath as I covered my mouth in disbelief that this was happening. God heard us! I just couldn't believe it. God showed me something that day. He showed me that he not only loved and cared for me, but also he loved and cared about the same things I did. He loved my children so much. I was softening more and more as God made himself irresistible. I felt him whittle away another portion of my heart. At that very moment, I felt so loved.

Alec went to church with us that Sunday, which happened to be Mother's Day. I was so excited for us all to be there as a family. As the pastor spoke, I looked over at Alec and watched his expression. He was paying attention with an intense look on his face. I knew he was listening, and every word spoken was soaking in. Near the end of service, the pastor asked if anyone wanted to be baptized. I almost fell out of my seat when Alec stood up and walked to the front. Was he serious? He was crying and ready to give his life to Jesus. What a Mother's Day gift! What an amazing family I had! God truly was watching over us, and he saved Alec.

The following week was brand new to us all. Alec and Airic

Alec being baptized by his stepdad, Tommy, and our pastor on May 8, 2011.

wanted to start a Bible study, and Tommy agreed to teach them in our living room. Alec invited his friend to join in. The next Bible study, Airic had some friends over as well. Within a few months, the numbers grew to over forty teens stampeding through our home to get to Jesus. Once a week our yard, our home, and our lives were invaded by young people hungry for God's Word. Some teens even showed up that no one knew. It was incredible!

I would watch Tommy share his heart with the young people, and I couldn't help but stare at Alec and Airic. I was looking at three brand new people, not to mention myself. I remember speaking to God in my heart: My God, look what you've done. I'm here with the greatest husband and sons anyone could ever ask for. I'm happy. More than happy, I'm free. I'm finally proud of who I am and what you've helped me grow to be. You only make me want to

Me, Alec, Tommy, and Airic

love you more. Oh, thank you, thank you for this life." My heart was full, and my family was secure.

Our Bible study quickly outgrew our house, so the mayor of our town invited us to use his building. So many young people came, and the group just kept growing. Alec would run out into the town looking for teenagers to scoop up and bring to Bible study. He and Airic were great and mighty warriors for God, and Tommy was not only their father but their pastor. Then our pastor asked Tommy and me to be the youth leaders at church, and we gladly accepted. One day a week we met with the youth in our town for Bible study, and on Sunday evenings we taught the youth at church. Things were happening so fast!

The church youth group numbers kept growing until finally a few of our church leaders recognized a calling on us that I don't think we even realized was happening. They wanted us to start our own church. They saw that we were strong leaders with a heart for not only the youth, but people in general. We loved to serve people and help wherever we were needed. Tommy and I prayed and talked about it. We wanted to be sure this was what God wanted us to do.

God wasted no time in giving us his answer. Within a week of this crazy idea being mentioned to us, we had a building, a sound system, and a handful of people to start this new journey with us. Legacy Church was born! We started in a building with a spare multipurpose room that comfortably seated fifty people. In the beginning, we had a keyboard, a djembe, three vocals, and a tiny speaker so everyone could hear the music. I still laugh about the beginning stages of our journey.

I'll never forget that stuffy room with the ugliest orange chairs I'd ever seen. Any time you'd sit down in one of those chairs, you were very likely going to get goosed. The metal was broken in spots, and I seemed to always get the chair that liked to take off my hide.

Our church continued growing at great numbers, and we had to move out of the multipurpose room to make room for more people and more volunteers to help out. The excitement was overwhelming, and I could barely believe how fast we were growing. It was the most insane thing I'd ever seen.

There Tommy and I were, both ordained as pastors, ready to lay down our lives for whatever God asked us to do. The question was: What was God really going to ask us to do? The answers were about to unfold. Since the leaders in our organization trained future pastors in Puerto Rico, I knew we'd be moving soon. I was willing but very afraid for my boys.

Then one day, Tommy called me on his way home from work. I knew it couldn't be good because it was way too early for him to have left work. He'd been working at a great job, but the company no longer needed his position. They told him they kept him as long as possible because they cared for him, but they could no longer justify the means to pay him. He was so afraid to call me with the news, but he assured me everything would be okay because he had already prepared many resumes. I believe he was as surprised as I was with what came out of my mouth next.

"Tommy, don't send out a single resume. You need to pastor our church fulltime and God will take care of everything else. It's time to put the sale sign in the front yard too."

I actually thought someone possessed me and started talking crazy nonsense. I was officially losing my mind. However, I knew what God was doing. God knew those directions needed to come from me to Tommy instead of the other way around in order for us both to agree. God has a way of reassuring us all.

The "for sale" sign was in the front yard for a whopping three days, and just like that, our house sold. Now what???

With the house sold, we started talking about leaving for training in Puerto Rico. Then our pastor said we would be the first pastors trained and ordained in Ohio where we lived. The organization had built a cabin out in the middle of nowhere for training purposes, and this would be our temporary home instead of Puerto Rico. This place was so new that an access road had not yet been built. The potential problems didn't end there, though. Alec and Airic attended an online school and needed internet access, and clearly there was no service out in the middle of nowhere. And I found out we couldn't take my dog, Lily, my little baby girl. Oh, I loved that silly knobby-headed Doberman.

I had many things to think about, but it wasn't a question of if I would make the move and do the training, but more along the lines of how to do it. I started out with laying hands on my dog. She stared at me with her beautiful amber eyes, and I prayed. "God, you made her for me. I love her. But I will go for you because you have need of me. All I ask is please, for me, find her a good home. I love her, Lord. I know you love her, too. You care about me so much that you also care about what I care about. Please send help."

The next dilemma we faced was the driveway. There was no way to put in a long driveway from the road to the cabin in time for us to move in. We needed a backup plan. So, here we were, with the heart of David running toward the giant. I felt as though the tools needed to defeat that giant were being taken away one at a time. God saw it as a different route. We started packing, knowing everything would be okay.

We talked to Tommy's mom, and she said it was fine for us to stay with her until we were able to find a place to live. We planned to stay upstairs and use two bedrooms and a bathroom. We had access to all she owned, of course, since it's hard to confine two young men to one bedroom.

We didn't have an income that could sustain us, so I worked at a nearby gas station and did a little work in online sales. The church was unable to pay us any income because it was still not bringing in enough money and the church rent came first. When we would start our training wasn't quite clear either. We had no idea how long we would be living with Tommy's mom or where we would go from there.

Isn't God so funny like this? We sold a house that we technically didn't need to sell because we were going to train where we were. We moved in with Tommy's mom, and guess what? The boys had internet access and then decided to go back to their local school until graduation. I also got to keep my knobby-headed fur baby! I did ask God why he felt the need for us to sell everything and move. Interestingly enough, his reply was this: "Shanda, I knew you'd always wonder if you would have given it all up for me. I wanted you to know personally that you would have. You were willing, and that's all I need. I'm searching for the willing, and you were."

Living out of boxes wasn't easy, but we were truly blessed. Tommy's mom made it so easy for us. She did all she could to help make our transition and move go as smoothly as possible. She may never know how much she is appreciated. (I hope in reading this, she can see how much she means to us.)

Sometimes, we think we can just grab someone by the hand and lead them straight to God. Perhaps that is true for a person interested in knowing God, but, without a foundation of who God is, that can be taxing not only on us but also the relationship we have with that person. Without a deep relationship, they can't truly trust us.

We had been living with Tommy's mom a little over a year when Alec started dating a young lady that wasn't exactly looking for Jesus. He had recently met her and she was very apprehensive about the whole idea of God. So, instead of Alec leading her, she, in fact, led him straight down a road he had no being business on.

The Bible says not to entertain love until it prospers. Solomon 8:4 says, "I charge you, O daughters of Jerusalem, do not stir up nor awaken love until it pleases." In other words, don't start something you aren't ready to finish; wait until it has grown into real love that you can forever live with. In Alec's relationship with this young lady, they were not ready at all. It took a turn for the worst and Alec started acting much like the company he was keeping. Bad behavior was surfacing quickly. He was drinking with his new friends, staying out late, and breaking curfew all the time.

He was old enough to make his own decisions without Tommy and me trying to run his life, but we still had rules for our house. He would constantly show up late and forget to lock the door at night, leaving us all in an unsafe environment. However, when we spoke to him about our concerns, he completely blew up. My heart was so broken to see such a strong young man with all his hopes and dreams of helping the world shattered to nothingness within a few weeks' time. The arguing got worse at home, and he grew very cold toward me, Airic, and Tommy.

One evening, he came home and walked into my room with a very contentious look on his face. I smiled and asked him how he was. He said only three words as he looked away from me in disgust.

"I'm moving out."

I was shocked. I knew he was upset, but this was the worst

thing he could do. He was leaving the only positive influence he had left. I didn't argue with him. I wanted to stop him, but I knew if I tried, it would just cause more fracas.

Tommy and I asked if he needed help getting his mattress and box springs down the stairs. He spitefully yanked and grabbed at the mattress, throwing it back and forth as he promptly refused our offer. I stood there helplessly frozen watching him struggle. Tommy, Airic, and I remained quiet as he grabbed what belongings he could. Unfortunately, his moving quickly into an apartment only helped his bad decisions add up. I heard rumors that he told people we had kicked him out because we didn't like his new girl-friend and we didn't agree with his lifestyle. (We had talked to him previously about obeying the rules and respecting the curfew we had given him.)

I knew the relationship he had with his girlfriend couldn't last. A relationship based on terms never does. He couldn't keep her happy. At least not for long. She was very needy, and I understood why. Her mother had abandoned her, and her father wasn't around much. She didn't have much upbringing and had zero respect for adults, let alone me.

Alec often called us needing money. I'd help here and there if I could. One particular time, he called, and we didn't have what he needed. His girlfriend called me a worthless mother, along with a few other words, to deepen the emotional dagger in my back that Alec allowed her to stab me with. Of course, I cried, but it wasn't because of the names I'd been called. It was the fact that my son needed my help, and I didn't have it to give to him. I was worthless. At least to me.

A few months went by, and it was over. Alec's relationship with his girlfriend ended terribly, and he was absolutely grief-stricken. I'm not sure if it was because he was heartbroken or plain prideful, but he refused to come home and allow us to help. That pride and independence led to a much deeper problem. With bigger problems come bigger decisions. With a broken heart, and no desire to heal it, comes the option fora remedial mental escape to alleviate the stress. The ability to escape the pain of heartbreak is much easier than approaching the root of the pain, and there are many colorful ways to outrun the agony. Oh, but misery always surfaces no matter how deeply we bury it. The symptoms of past hurts will always leak through the crevices of our lives. Alec started using drugs once again, and this time it was worse than the first time. He stayed with random friends, asked us for money, and treated us with complete disrespect. He started losing large amounts of weight even though he couldn't afford to lose much since he was already tall and slender.

I started worrying for not only his safety, but our own as well. Whenever he needed money, he would randomly pull into our driveway with some of the biggest drug dealers in the city. They now knew where we lived. I clearly remember the day he walked up the sidewalk as if he owned the place and banged on the door as if we were late on our rent. The look on his face was nothing I'd ever seen.

"Mom, if you love me at all, you'll give me some cash." He continued to say other hurtful things as I stood there taking in every blow.

I stared intensely at him. I knew what he wanted the cash for.

His dealers were sitting in my driveway. Then I made one of the hardest decisions of my life. I refused my boy.

"I can feed you. You're welcome to come in and eat whatever you want." I puffed my chest to show no fear. "But I'm not giving you any money."

He screamed he hated me, slammed the door in my face, and left with those men that he did not belong with.

I fell to my knees sobbing as tears streamed down my face. My boy was in danger, and I was helpless. I didn't think I would make it as long as I did without crying, but I knew I needed to stay firm with Alec. Airic and Tommy ran to me to try and comfort me. They hated watching me cry, but I couldn't help it. That's all I did. Airic always tried to protect me in any way he could, and if I cried, he would run to me to console me. I strived to be strong in front of my children, but this was far too much to bear.

Because Tommy and I were very concerned for Airic's safety, we had to make the most paradoxical decision. We weren't sure if Alec and his friends would return and try to hurt Airic. In order to protect him, we told him he needed to start carrying a weapon. This was only in case Alec would come around high, in a state of confusion, making it possible for Airic to be in harm's way. I can't explain what that decision felt like. I stood there handing my one son a knife to protect him from my other son that I loved just as much. I wanted to be sick. What was I supposed to do? Was this right? What if Alec attacks his brother because he can't control himself on drugs? If Airic isn't protected, he could die. If Alec is hurt, he could die. Frankly, the thought of any of this made me want to die. How do you choose between sons? I felt like I was being made to choose.

Weeks went by, and then I received a phone call out of the blue to let me know Alec was staying with a few of my closest relatives. I was furious and relieved at the same time. I hadn't heard from him for weeks, and I had feared he was dead. I had no idea if he was lying in a ditch somewhere, and the news had been kept from me. Every call and every knock at the door had me on edge and held me tightly to Fear's side. I never knew if I'd get the call every mother dreads.

When my relative called, they told me Alec was dating a new young lady named Chloe and she seemed very nice. They seemed hesitant to tell me much more, so I began to probe with questions. I asked how Alec was doing. I asked if they knew where he was staying. There was a pause on the other end of the phone followed by a short sigh. I knew what that meant. Unfortunately, they weren't calling with great news. Alec had been running pills for another family member. When he had gone to make a delivery, the man he went with stole all the pills Alec had been given to sell. This left Alec with no money or pills to return to his dealer. The family member, his dealer, was irate. He screamed at Alec that family doesn't betray family. All that meant was "there is no money OR drugs for me," so he punished my son. Alec was beaten for his failure to make the sale. My heart sank. I felt every ounce of blood drain from my body. I went limp and hung up the phone.

I just couldn't believe my own family could do this. I'm supposed to trust them. They are the ones I'm supposed to be able to call and lean on during times like these. What were they thinking? They could have had my son killed. I gripped my bedside blankets, calling out to God, but nothing came out. I could only groan from the deepest part of my soul. I couldn't speak. I just wept for my little boy. I pictured him in my mind as I cried. I just kept seeing my baby. He wasn't a grown man failing me and failing God. He was my little man. He was my sweet blonde-haired, blue-eyed baby boy, and he needed my help. Except there was nothing I could do to help him.

The phone rang again. I stared at it before I decided to answer. Tears flowed like rivers down my face as I answered. I took a deep breath and said hello. It was one of the relatives hiding my son. They knew I was aware and thought they could smooth it over with me. My face changed its countenance as I composed myself. I never felt so calm in my life as I said to this person, "I can't speak to you about this right now. I need to pray. I need to ask God how to do this. Give me three days."

Why I chose three days is still beyond me, but I knew if I spoke right then and there, all hell would have broken loose and I would not have displayed my Father's love at all. Words would have been slung like mud. My statement asking for time provoked my relative to complete and utter disgust. They told me that I wasn't a Christian because I couldn't forgive and that I was ungodly and had no right to judge them. I said nothing else except to tell them that it was better for them that I prayed. And I hung up the phone.

Isn't it incredible that people still use what we call "The Jesus Card"? This card is best used when someone is in need from a person who claims to love Jesus. When the Christian is asked to act a certain way or do a certain thing but won't succumb to the request, the victim feels as if they aren't being treated fairly. People assume just because a Christian isn't able to meet their expectations that the Christian couldn't possibly love Jesus and, therefore, is a judgmental hypocrite. Some people assume just because a Christian loves the Lord that they have no common sense and will do what everybody wants. That's plain manipulation.

After hanging up the phone, I stood there feeling naked and paralyzed with grief. I felt as if I'd been beaten to near death in front of all the world. I stood there as if they all watched me with blank faces. Alone. Naked. Beaten. Left for dead. No one cared to help. No one wanted to rescue me. I needed answers. I needed God to help me. But all I heard was utter silence. It felt like God had pulled an iron veil between the two of us. I felt like I was trapped in a glass, sound-proof room, almost as if I knew God could see me and could read my lips but refused to respond. I knew he heard me but wasn't answering. This time, I was certain of God's presence. It was different than years gone by when I wondered if God was really there. Now, I felt as though he was just staring at me. I knew he had all the answers I needed.

"Is Alec ok? Will he come home? God, is my son going to die?"

Still, nothing. Silence was all I heard. For the first time in my life, I could describe silence as deafening. It was as if a bomb was detonated, yet there was nothing but dead noise. I could hear the sounds of a cave crying out with loneliness. I was nothing but a hollow pit, a woman in grave clothes. Little did I know, God was about to speak louder than I had ever heard him. It was time to make the sacrifice. It was time to lay my Isaac down.

10

My Isaac

God! God!
Help!

There it is. That was my lengthy prayer. What else could I say? Help is what I needed, and help was all I wanted. I needed to hear God plainly, and I begged him for help. It was time to "lay my Isaac down."

I was reminded of a story in the Bible about a man named Abraham. He was promised great things from God. One of those promises involved his son named Isaac. Abraham loved Isaac with all his heart. One day the Lord asked Abraham to take his son up to the land of Moriah to sacrifice Isaac as a burnt offering on the mountains. Abraham, without question, got up early the next day, saddled a donkey, and took two of his servants and his son where God told him to go. After the three-day journey, Abraham saw the place where God wanted him to be. Abraham told his servants to stay there with the donkey because he and his son were going to travel a little further to worship God.

Isaac carried the wood for the fire while Abraham carried the knife. Isaac knew they had the wood and the knife, so he asked his father where the sheep for the sacrifice was. "God will provide" was Abraham's answer. When they reached their destination, Abraham tied his son, laid him on the altar, and picked up the knife to kill Isaac.

"Abraham! Abraham!" God called to him. "Don't lay a hand on the lad, or do anything to harm him; for now I know that you fear God, since you have not withheld your son, your only son, from me."

Abraham lifted his eyes and saw a ram, the sacrifice God provided. God promised more blessings to Abraham and his descendants that day because Abraham remained faithful and trusted God.

It was so hard to lay my Isaac on the altar and leave the outcome up to God. For years, I thought Abraham was the bravest man alive to do such a thing. But Abraham had faith. Abraham wasn't afraid because he remembered the words God had spoken and the promise God made for his son, Issac. Turns out, he trusted God and knew God couldn't kill his son because he had made Abraham a promise. Abraham figured that even if he murdered the boy, God would have needed to bring him back in order to fulfill the promises. All Abraham had to do was trust and show up. God supplied the sacrifice. After all, a promise is a promise if it's from God. Now it was my turn to trust God. I had my son, the wood, and the knife. Now the real question was if I would trust the Lord to keep his promises to me the way Abraham trusted. I was about to find out.

The phone rang again. The caller was a very concerned man of the law warning us that they had picked up Alec. I was undone. No! No! No! This could not be happening.

A few days went by before Alec contacted me and Tommy wanting us to meet him at a nearby location. When we arrived, he wasn't acting right. He was frazzled, irrational, and paranoid. He kept repeating that he thought we were with the police. It was clear he was high, but we had to act like we knew nothing. We coaxed him into trusting us enough to come home and talk.

He spilled it all. I'd never seen him so afraid. He told us he was very high and scared he was dying because he didn't know what he took. We offered to get him help, and he agreed because he was in such fear of losing his life. We immediately drove him to the hospital and handed the substance to a doctor to identify what it was. The doctor returned and told us that it was meth. They gave Alec something to help relax him, and he fell asleep quickly.

Over the next few days, we were all on pins and needles. Alec started to talk to us, and his mind cleared. He told us the police did show up at a campsite to arrest him and his friends a few days prior to his contacting us. He was unsure what happened that night and refused to tell the police anything. At least his mind had been clear enough to know not to say a word without a lawyer present.

Weeks passed, and Alec was determined to get his life together. I saw his beautiful, sober face daily, and I felt much safer. Yet, I wondered what the police were up to. We didn't know the severity of Alec's situation. None of us knew what to expect. My mind was in constant turmoil from thoughts. Were the police going to drop the charges? Were there even any charges filed? Should we call the courthouse and try to rattle chains? Should we stay quiet so we don't bring attention to Alec? We sat there in suspense praying the situation would just go away.

Then, there it was—a knock at the door. This knock didn't even sound like a regular knock. I stood up as if I knew. When I opened the door, a police officer handed me papers addressed to Alec. He was being charged with a felony for manufacturing meth and facing three to five years in prison.

I stood there with a whole new fear in my heart. How can this ever be God's will? How does this get better? God gave me this child, and now I may lose him. I believed everything I had poured into my boy was all in vain. All my heart and soul devoted to my boy was gone. My son was either facing prison time or leaving for the military. Alec had told me and Tommy that he wanted to start over, and he had been talking with a recruiter ever since he had been released from the hospital. I tried to believe he wanted a clean slate to work with. I'm certain he did want a fresh start, but as his mother, I knew he was running away. He said the recruiter was feeling pretty good about everything. Well, I wasn't. I was appalled and in shock. I had to talk with God! I prepared my case and was determined to get answers.

There I was, sitting on the world's most uncomfortable futon, upstairs in my bedroom/living room ready to contend for answers. I sat there with bitter tears streaming down my face. I wanted to know what God intended on doing. I said smugly, "What will it be, God? Prison or the military? Will he be in prison afraid for his life daily? Oh, the things of horror in my mind, God! Make it stop! Maybe you will have him go to the military and possibly die in battle."

Even if he went into the military, to me, no honor given to any man is enough to appease such a broken heart. No flag could replace the hole in my life if Alec sacrificed his life on the battle-field. Only pain would remain.

Then, I opened the floodgates of my soul. "Oh, God what will you do? Why did you give me this son? Was it for him to die in front of me? I rather you kill me. Are you trying to kill me? The chance of losing my son is so enormous, I'd rather you kill me now! I mean it, God! Just do it! Why do you give one man a set of won-derful parents and let the other man remain an orphan? Why me? What makes you pick and choose? Why does Tommy have such wonderful parents that love him softly, with tender care, and here I am? Here am I! What will it be? Prison or the military?"

I couldn't help but think to myself "what else was there?" There weren't exactly a lot of other options appearing before us. It wasn't long before I felt God's presence. I knew God wanted to talk with me. What he was about to say, I'd never make up myself nor be capable of making up. God answered me.

"Those are my choices, Shanda? The two? That is what you've condensed me to—two choices? I Am God! Where were you when I hung the moon? How about the earth spinning on nothing? I placed the stars where they are and spoke to the waters to tell them where to stop on the shoreline. But, you...you have given me these two choices. You must know that he is NOT your son. He was my son first, and I lent him to you to raise. I love him more than you could ever fathom. He's my son, and I love him so much. I chose you for your parents and your parents for you. You are to go and tell the world the love I have shown you. The mercy I have given to you is to be shared with the world because I want them to meet me. They need to see me through you. Make no mistake...I make NO mistakes. Don't put me into a box. I am God, and you will see me do miracles."

I sat there silent, taking short breaths from his presence. I felt so chastened and yet so very loved. I was in awe of God. He was in control, and everything would be fine.

Tommy, Alec, Alec's new girlfriend Chloe, and I walked into the first court meeting to see where everything stood. The police checked us in as they do, and they asked Alec's girlfriend her name. We thought it odd, but she told them. They told Chloe there was a warrant for her arrest because she failed to show for her hearing. She pleaded with them to believe her that she never received the papers.

Immediately, I stepped in between Chloe and the officer on duty. I told the officer that she was not going to arrest my soon-to-be daughter-in-law. Lo and behold, they searched for the papers and spoke with the judge to have another hearing at a later time. They let her go, and I just held her in my arms and we cried. I don't know what made me stand in the middle of Chloe and the law, but I spoke with a whole new authority. I didn't speak with anger or attitude but with God's authority.

As we approached the court, we sensed that everyone was very angry and not afraid to treat Alec like a criminal. The prosecutor addressed Alec with a cocky statement:

"When the court finds you guilty—"

"IF he is found guilty." I quickly interrupted the prosecutor.

"Alec is innocent until proven guilty. That's the country I live in."

The prosecutor stared at me with a death stare as if he'd like to execute me slowly. He got down to my eye level where I sat on a bench. He said quietly, yet carelessly, "It's parents like you that make me sick. You condone this and try to cover this up by bailing them out and you only make more criminals."

I didn't speak. I couldn't. Had I spoken to him, I'd have been heading to jail myself and dishonoring God. I wanted to tell him in desperation that he knew nothing! I wanted to tell him he had no idea about the times I had held my child's feet for hours after he came home from an eight-day binge on meth. I held those feet close to me, and as he slept, I prayed. I prayed for hours over his precious, dirty, scrawny feet. I held them as if it were the first and last time I might ever hold them. I wanted to scream at the prosecutor with rage about how I had been in a fetal position on the floor broken for my son on more occasions than I cared to remember. But, what did that prosecutor know, anyways?

I felt the prosecutor was numb to all the hurt hiding behind the eyes of every case. I thought that maybe my son was just another case number, ready to be sealed with "The One No One Cares About" stamp. But he wasn't another case. He wasn't another statistic. He was my baby! He was my son and the son of a big God! The prosecutor was talking about my little boy that cried if he were scolded because he was heartbroken to think he disappointed someone. He had boo-boos and loved to play outside. He had a huge heart and loved to love. He was more than this. No one knew him like I knew him. This is what I saw when I looked at my boy. I needed so desperately for them to see him that way—the way Jesus sees us all with his merciful eyes and innocent verdict.

I stood up to walk into the restroom to pray. I was desperate. As soon as the door shut behind me, I called the angels. "I want twelve angels to go into the room with Alec. I want you all to speak to the police, speak to the judge, and speak to prosecutors! Change their minds. Find him not guilty. Whisper to all the police officers that are there to testify against my son. Go now!"

Then I asked God to honor my word. I knew I was allowed to summon the angels to minister for me based on Hebrews 1. We are made higher than the angels because of God's son. I know I'm made just like Jesus, and I have inherited everything he owns including the charge over angels to do the will of God and help on my behalf.

We left the courthouse that day not knowing that it would be a year and a half before another hearing.

During the time between the hearings, I had to stay steady when I wanted to crumble. Then we received some wonderful news. Alec and Chloe told us she was pregnant. We were so happy. To me, the baby was a new life and a new beginning. I already absolutely loved that little life inside Chloe's tiny tummy.

However, a fear occasionally rushed over me. What would happen if both Alec and Chloe went to prison? Would I get my grandbaby until they were released? Will she have the baby in prison? Will the baby get to see its parents? Oh my, the thoughts that tormented me.

Alec was working for the town until his verdict came through, so we took Chloe to her routine baby checkup appointments. One particular day, Chloe gave a urine sample to make sure her hormone levels were rising. The nurse came in with the worst news. She stated that Chloe's HCG levels were not rising and were decreasing, the sign of a miscarriage. I wanted to say so many things to Chloe. I wanted to hold her and tell her how sorry I was. I was watching her die inside with every minute that passed by, not knowing if her baby would make it. I was devastated.

Chloe called me up days later, sobbing. I knew. Tears rushed down my cheeks as she told me that my grandbaby was gone. All I could think was I would see my grandbaby one day. I wondered what they looked like. Was it a little boy? Was it a little girl? Why, God? Then the real flooding of thoughts came. Was it because Alec and Chloe were going to jail, and this was God's way? How ridiculous of a thought, but I was thinking it.

We all want answers to life's most tragic moments. So much so that we will make up whatever we can to either self soothe or blame someone. This is where God takes the brunt of it all. I was trying so hard not to be angry, but I was. What could I have done to have deserved all this? What did Alec and Chloe do to deserve the loss of their child? Is this a punishment? What sick test was this? This was not the character of my God. I do know this. My faith was shaking to the point of overthrow. I was breaking a little more every day.

Unfortunately, Alec received some heartbreaking news on top of this tragedy. He received a call from his recruiter. They saw the felony charges and dismissed him as a candidate. He was devastated. I saw tears in his eyes that spoke to me in single words— Failure. Defeated. Worthless. Insufficient. He felt like he had no purpose even though he was trying to make a better life for himself. Well, isn't there supposed to be a happy ending to these kinds of stories? If you change, don't you live happily ever after? These are real consequences in a real world.

※

It was time. It was time for Alec's verdict. I prayed, "Here we go, God. What are you able to do with this broken mess? You told me you are God and you can do anything." I was about to see muscle behind the God I called Father.

We went directly into the courtroom when we arrived. We sat there in silence, and I watched carefully. I watched everyone shuffling their papers and tapping their pens on the desk.

"All rise."

The judge walked in, and my breath seemed to become shallow. I tried to control it as if I were on trial and didn't want them to see me shaking. We sat down again, and I listened intently. The judge had a kind face. I felt a warmth coming from him, and at first, I thought I was just imagining it. I wanted it to all go away, so at this point, I truly couldn't trust my emotions.

The judge called the officer that arrested Alec. Oh, God, here it was…

With kind eyes, the officer looked at my son and said, "Sir, he doesn't belong here." He stated a few other things and was dismissed. I was in shock.

Then it was the prosecutor's turn to state what the facts were. He too stated that Alec should not be there. He was smiling at Alec as he made those statements.

I was about to fall over! In my head of a thousand thoughts, I was thinking, "Am I losing my mind? Do they know they are saying the opposite of what they said before?"

The judge smiled at Alec and told him that he could tell he was a good kid. He told him that he was charged with a misdemeanor, and he needed to do community service. He looked at Tommy and then back at Alec before stating that he could even work in his father's church to fulfill his hours. Plus he told Alec that he was completely waiving the court fee.

I sat there with my mouth wide open and in absolute shock. I could feel God's love. I sometimes still picture God standing over my shoulder that day saying "Ahem, option three."

A few months passed by, and Alec and Chloe came to us with wonderful news. They were pregnant again. I was elated! Chloe's case had been thrown out, and they were both free. God was restoring their lives. Then they called us one September day to tell us they wanted to elope. We were to tell no one. We rushed to a scenic lake in the area and, there on the shore, they were united under heaven in the presence of me, my husband, and God. What a perfect day!

I never told my family about all the pain we endured during Alec's drug abuse and subsequent court cases. Not too long ago, I finally told my sister Jennifer about the twelve angels that I asked to go into the courtroom. As I told her the story, the strangest thing happened. I stopped mid-sentence and heard God tell me a secret. Jennifer asked me what was wrong, and I smiled.

"God just told me why he had me ask him to send twelve angels. I never knew why, and he just told me."

"What did he say?"

I choked out the words with tears in my eyes. "He told me 'There are twelve in a jury, Shanda. I sent them in to judge your son according to my Word. I rendered him innocent.'"

Tears streamed down both our faces in amazement at all that had happened.

Life is so crazy sometimes. I have realized that we all have an "Isaac" or two in our lives. Maybe it's not our children. Maybe it's our work. Maybe it's our spouse that we need to trust God with. Maybe it's our life in general. Do you have an "Isaac" in your life that needs to be laid down?

11

God, I Forgive You

God,

I know you've always known me. Before the foundation of the world, you knew my name. I was so angry at you for so many years. I felt betrayed and disregarded. I wanted to rid the hate and unforgiveness in people, myself, and, what I thought for years—in you. I had to let go of all the hurt. I had to trust you. I have seen your hand on my life. Through all the suffering and life-changing events, I am still learning how to let go of a little every day.

I am now willing to see you, unveiled face and outstretched arms. You have had so much mercy on me and my bruised heart. You have taken everything I have been through and made it for good. You waste nothing. I am so glad to have met the real you. I never knew I could be so loved.

God, I ask you to forgive me of my unbelief in myself and in you. Although you have never sinned or done anything deserving the need to be forgiven, you have been so merciful, patient, and longsuffering with me. You have loved me enough to even let me say: "God, I forgive you." Amen.

I can start by saying that I never should have made it. I shouldn't even be alive. All I was to everyone was another small-town statistic. I was an attention-seeking little girl hoping for each day to just be a little better than the one before. A young girl with a ninth-grade education doesn't make it too far in this world, but God had other plans.

Satan saw my potential and wanted me dead. God knew my potential and saw to it that I not only lived but lived in such a way that it confounded the wise. He took a beaten girl and made her unbeatable. I was weak and afraid, yet today I composed a letter of great news to encourage you. I am more than a washed-out misfit. I am a conqueror of not one but many wars that were fought for me by my Father.

People sometimes remind me of the horror that I saw, but I stand here today to tell you of the miracles God has shown me. I look at my mother and thank God she is here. I could have lost her that night along with many other nights. He let me keep her. I could have lost my two sisters. I couldn't imagine my life without them. I could have lost Tommy to my selfish ways. I could have lost Airic, but he stood in his faith. I could have lost Alec to drugs, but God had other plans.

God taught me that he wants to be a part of my life, not just an idea. He wants me to live at my fullest, not just barely make it. He wants me to thrive, not just survive. My goal is heaven on earth. This life isn't about just making it to heaven; death is not the way out. God doesn't want death to be my savior; he is my savior. He wants me to show the world all he is and all he has for everyone.

As you are reading this, I am imparting a gift. I see scales falling off your eyes as they did for Paul when he went to see Ananias. These scales, whether they are condemnation or law, cause us to see the world through a blurry kaleidoscope. I just wonder if we realize where the scales came from. Think back to the Garden of Eden and remember who was with Eve the day she questioned her identity—the serpent of old. He doesn't want you to know who you are. He doesn't care if you believe in God or him. He only needs to keep you a little tipped on the scale of pure identity. He knows the moment you see clearly who you are, he is done for. Satan wants to give you his thoughts. He has no original thoughts of his own. He is so jealous of you and me. He doesn't understand why God finds us so astounding.

Believe me when I tell you that you really are astounding. You can make it. You were designed to do more than make it. You only need to believe it. There's so much awaiting you. Let's link arms and pray for one another.

On the next page is a prayer God inspired me to write to women everywhere. This prayer can be directed to men as well. When I wrote this prayer, I knew I needed to say this out loud for even Satan to hear. I don't condone having a conversation with Satan, but there are times he needs to remember who we are. I needed to hear myself say it. I also needed to be reminded who and whose I was.

The Virtuous Woman Prayer

I wake up this day to call it mine. Mine only because it was granted to me by One mightier than the one trying to take it.

I will not break stride. I will not bow down. I won't slow to the pain of life's thrusting trials. I will press onward. I will push through the guilt of past reminders and cut through the thicket of life's future fears. I will not allow you, small god, to take flight over my mind and dive inward to take hold. I may flail my arms upward in what looks like surrender, but that's the moment that I'm reaching for God. I will never shout "I'm through!" Even though the tears come, I will brush them away with the Hand that doesn't belong to me, because God prepares my path to see. \

You may think I'm overtaken when your breath is in my nostrils and we are standing toe to toe, but there is One greater who breathed in it before you knew me. You may see my knees weak and bending, and you'll be right because they are bending to a savior mightier than all kings set before you.

I will not stop.

I will not be conquered.

I will overcome.

He sees you and knows my name. This is the part where you run!

I pray this prayer this morning to my God. This is my prayer of thanks for I am a great woman of virtue standing with sword in hand and armor of God in place. I am the pen of a ready writer awaiting my page.

In Jesus' name I pray.

Amen

A Letter to the Reader

Dearest friend,

My hope in writing this book was to show you how the heart of that same child cried out to God just as I do today. I wrote each chapter with a true prayer that came directly from my mouth. You will notice that, though they may not have been with eloquent words, they carried the nature of a child with a true heart. I followed each prayer with what was happening during that moment in time. I pray you realize that, upon the unveiling of each chapter, I portrayed every stage in my life as changing, just as each experience was growing me into the woman I am today.

I wrote this book with the intention and hope that you would meet Jesus if you have not already met him. I pray that you know you are not alone. You are not here to figure all of this out and trudge through life with no help. You have a Helper.

You must see yourself as more than enough. You are worth living for and worth dying for. You are so very loved, and there is a great purpose for you. You are needed as God's hands and feet. The body is crying out, awaiting your arrival. Never let anyone tell you that you must earn your way to your Father's heart. He earned it for you. Relationship over religion will always melt the Father's heart. He looks at you as innocent, and you are deemed holy, blameless, spotless, and without blemish. You are as God is.

I pray for you, my reader, and want you to know I also love you. I trust you will see it's possible to be angry at God and not even realize it. I was. Oh, but when you meet the real Jesus, your life will change in an instant.

It sounds so appalling to some of my readers' ears to even hear the words "God, I forgive you." Some of you may even feel it's a bit temerarious. Maybe it is a bit reckless, although we tend to do those sorts of things from time to time, don't we? Please keep in mind that although the title is, well…offensive, it reflects my true feelings during my life. An angry person must forgive, right? Even if that forgiveness is directed toward a perfect God. We will find out soon enough that we are angry with a character we conjured up in our own minds. We want to blame someone to make the pain and loss all go away. We only need to meet the Father, the real Jesus.

I started writing this book years ago with the intention of having it completed in just a few months. Much to my surprise, God had other plans. Throughout the entire writing of this book, God whittled away bit by bit at my heart. There was and still remains a great work to be done in me.

I lost my Lily Girl several months back. She seemed skittish and had grown lumps in her throat. We took her to the vet, and they ran tests showing no cancer. It was best I didn't know or I would have felt the need to put her down. She didn't suffer the symptoms, nor was she tired long. She was my "Promise Dog." My immortal girl went to sleep suddenly in Tommy and my arms. She stood up, and with one big breath, she lay on the couch. I held her little face and Tommy held her chest as she breathed her last. I couldn't even look at this book after Lily left us. I was so devastated and needed God to heal my heart.

A few chapters before the end, my Grammy was hospitalized for what we believed was pneumonia, and then she passed away. While Tommy and I were in the room saying goodbye, she muttered the words, "Honey, I'm ready, and I want to go home. Take me home." She said those words over and over. I knew she was not talking to us. She was talking to God, her True Love. She was most proud of my book and was so excited that I was speaking out. She wanted her story told. She wanted my mother's story told. She wanted my story told. Most of all, Grammy wanted the love of God told.

God sent his only Son to die in our place in order to save a broken, angry world. He was the ultimate sacrifice. Jesus. It's all about him. It's always been about him. My friends, it will always be about him, and you are as God is.

So, with all my heart and all my love, go and finish this race.

Forever Yours,
Shanda Miller

I'd say this is the end...
But it's only the beginning.

Acknowledgments

This book was greatly inspired by so many people.

This book wouldn't be complete without an acknowledgment of some of the finest literary geniuses I could have ever hoped to work with. Kara Starcher was the most gifted editor helping give my story rhythm and shape. Rob Coburn of Total Fusion Publishing helped ease all my fears about releasing my book, answered all my questions, and quieted my insecurities. I thank you all for being with me on this journey. I couldn't have done it without you.

I'd like to mention my Grammy. I can truly say she was my mentor throughout the years. If I can be half the woman she was, I know my Father will gladly say, "Well done, my good and faithful servant." I thank her for all she sacrificed to make sure her children and grandchildren were well taken care of by God. I know thousands of prayers reached the heavens from her cries.

I want to thank my mother, Janet, for my life. Through all the abuse and betrayal others bestowed upon her, she never gave up. Through faults and failures, she never stopped loving us and wanting nothing but the best life we could live. For that, I could never thank her enough for all she has given and given up. I love you, Mom.

To my darling children, Alec and Airic—My whole world was exposed to true love from you alone. You have caused me to strive for more when I didn't think I could go on. You've never stopped loving me even when I failed you. I have and always will love you endlessly and unconditionally. I've watched you grow from little boys that break things to men that build things. You both have given me and Tommy beautiful grandchildren—sweet Arria, my tiny apostle and future worship leader; wonderful Drevena, my fiery evangelist; Sophia darling, my angelic prophetess; and perhaps more to come. Thank you for giving us two beautiful daughters-in-law, Chloe and Megan, that love you and the Lord. I love you, my beautiful boys.

My daughters, Chloe and Megan—there are no words to describe how much you have filled my heart with love. You are true daughters to me, and I thank you for that. Thank you for being great women of virtue and always taking care of your husbands.

To the greatest teacher, example, and friend I could have ever hoped for—There are not words written to explain the love and respect that I have for you. Only heaven could hold the exposition of how I truly feel. You have been the perfect example of how God truly loves his bride. You've loved me with an intense and fierce passion. You've prayed over me with anointed hands time and time again. You've breathed Holy Spirit inspired words over me as I slept. Even when I was falling apart, there you were washing me with the water of the Word as I wanted to give up. You never quit. You persevered just as your Father persevered to the cross. He was willing to carry my sins, take on my shame, and cover me as you have done. Thank you for being steadily directed and dedicated to your family. With all the heartfelt gratitude a wife could give to her beloved, I thank you. I love you so much, Tommy Lee Miller. This, my love, is only the beginning. Let's run!

Me and my beloved, Tommy

When My Grandpa Gets to Heaven

Written by Shanda Miller

Dear Jesus,
When my grandpa gets to heaven,
I hope it's not a task.
There's just a few more favors
That I really need to ask.
The first request I'm asking,
I hope You understand.
Could You please build my grandpa
A giant Disneyland?
A big supply of Pepsi
With a Snickers candy bar.
Let him speed on heaven's streets
In his old-fashioned car.
I know he'd never ask You,
But I don't think he would care
If you would take his ball cap
And replace it with some hair.
Please, go outside with Grandpa.
Play some baseball and You'll see,
I know he always likes it,
Cause he always did with me.
But, when I get to Heaven,
I cannot wait to see
The rollercoaster made from God

For Grandpa and for me.
Please, keep my grandpa happy,
And always make him smile.
That worked for me and I may not see
My grandpa for a while.
When my grandpa gets to heaven,
I know that You will see
The reason that I tried to keep
My grandpa here with me.
Love,
Alec and Airic

Airic and Megan   Alec and Chloe

A Healing
Help Guide

Do I need to forgive?

Do I need to forgive someone?

"And be kind to one another, tenderhearted, forgiving one another, even as God in Christ forgave you." (Ephesians 4:32)

Forgiveness isn't a reflection of the worthiness of the person you are forgiving; forgiveness is a reflection of the person that forgave you.

How do I forgive myself?

Much like the answer above, we can't look at ourselves to see if we're worth forgiving. We have to look closely at the price of our forgiveness and determine if the blood of the perfect Son of God was sufficient for our blamelessness! If we disagree when it comes to forgiving ourselves, then we disagree with the sufficiency of the sacrifice of Jesus.

Is forgiveness a choice?

Much like love, forgiveness is a choice. We need to re-appropriate our ideology of forgiveness from the faculty of our emotion to the faculty of our will. Forgiveness doesn't always "feel" right. but forgiveness is right. We forgive because we choose to. (See the passage below.)

"Then He said to the disciples, 'It is impossible that no offenses should come, but woe to him through whom they do come! It would be better for him if a millstone were hung around his neck, and he were thrown into the sea, than that he should offend one of these little ones. Take heed to yourselves. If your brother sins against you, rebuke him; and if he repents, forgive him. And if he sins against you seven times in a day, and seven times in a day returns to you, saying, 'I repent,' you shall forgive him.'

And the apostles said to the Lord, 'Increase our faith.'

So the Lord said, "If you have faith as a mustard seed, you can say to this mulberry tree, 'Be pulled up by the roots and be planted in the sea,' and it would obey you. And which of you, having a servant plowing or tending sheep, will say to him when he has come in from the field, 'Come at once and sit down to eat'? But will he not rather say to him, 'Prepare something for my supper, and gird yourself and serve me till I have eaten and drunk, and afterward you will eat and drink'? Does he thank that servant because he did the things that were commanded him? I think not. So likewise you, when you have done all those things which you are commanded, say, 'We are unprofitable servants. We have done what was our duty to do.'" (Luke 17:1–10)

Jesus just taught a group of disciples that it doesn't take feelings or faith to forgive. As a recipient of the grace and forgiveness of God, forgiveness is now a gift that we have received that we can choose to pass on. Jesus refers to the forgiveness of a transgressor as the "duty" of one of His servants.

Repentance—What is it?

Confusion regarding exactly what repentance is can cause some serious trauma.

When I say "repent," what's the first thing you think of? For me, it's a man with a big voice making me feel bad for everything I've done. "Repentance" would be what he commands me to do after shaming me for what I've done. Repentance is when I feel so sorry for hurting God and I will try to stop doing the bad things I was doing. Right?

Well…not exactly. For people like you and me, repentance is actually way more than that. It's more powerful; it's more transformative; and it's healing. Repentance is how we access what God has for us. When Jesus preached, he said, "Repent, for the Kingdom of God is at hand!"

One of the easiest ways to misinterpret the Scriptures is to assume that a word in the Old Testament and a word in the New Testament have the same meaning. The word repent in the New Testament was a completely different concept than in the Old Testament. Repent in Greek is the word metanoeo meaning "to change one's mind." Jesus's commandment to repent was a commandment to change old thinking patterns and to develop a mind like his. We have the mind of Christ! You don't have to think the way you used to because you're no longer governed by the things that broke you!

Is God mad at me?

I realize that a relationship with someone will always determine how you interpret them. In Genesis, God said, "Don't eat of the tree of knowledge of Good and Evil lest you die." Because I had been taught that God was a mean and wrath-filled God and was waiting for me to step out of line so He could judge me, I didn't hear Him say, "Don't eat that tree or you'll die." I heard, "Don't eat that tree or I'll kill you."

When I thought about my oldest granddaughter heading directly for an electrical outlet with a metal house key in her hand, I understood the heart of my Father. When I think of my babies doing something I know will harm their future, my heart screams, "Don't do that or you'll be hurt!" I realized then that my Father has never been mad at me. He has dedicated his every effort to have a relationship with me and to protect me. He came as the high priest, he came as the cloud, he came as a pillar of fire, and he came as a man. He ultimately made his home in me after relentlessly pursuing me with his prodigal, passionate love.

What's my purpose?

It's becoming a well-known fact that statistically higher cases of depression are linked to nihilism or the thought process that produces no meaning for your existence. People don't want to live because they aren't sure they can find a reason to. Thankfully, our Father was very clear about why he breathed life into us. The first two chapters of Genesis are "the seed" of our created purpose and destiny! As long as you understand this, you'll never have to spend another day wondering if you're needed. You are!

"Then God said, 'Let Us make man in Our image, according to Our likeness; let them have dominion over the fish of the sea, over the birds of the air, and over the cattle, over all the earth and over every creeping thing that creeps on the earth.' So God created man in His own image; in the image of God He created him; male and female He created them. Then God blessed them, and God said to them, 'Be fruitful and multiply; fill the earth and subdue it; have dominion over the fish of the sea, over the birds of the air, and over every living thing that moves on the earth.'" (Genesis 1:26-28)

After reading that passage, you can see that God's original intention was not to create subjects to rule over, but sons and daughters in his image to rule with! Our life is proposed to manifest the nature of God in every aspect of human existence—fruitfulness, multiplication, advancement, and dominion. His desire is that we become his bodily, physical representation on this earth and his co-regent and governor in his visible creation. You will never be without a purpose or a mission.

A word of caution: this mandate follows you wherever you go.

It's easy to sometimes mistake the mission with the purpose. I've felt the pain of an "empty nest" and wondered what I should be doing with my life. I've seen the throws of employment—job today, none tomorrow. If you mistake your mission with your purpose, you will feel empty at the end of a season. Your never-changing purpose is to be the physical visible representation of Jesus to the world in your next mission!

How do I handle harsh words from others?

As a wise man once said, "Let the words of others be nothing to you. For what does killing a dead man do?"

My son Airic wrote those words based on Galatians 6:14—"As for me, may I never boast about anything except the cross of our Lord Jesus Christ. Because of that cross, my interest in this world has been crucified, and the world's interest in me has also died." (NLT)

When we change our minds about who we really are, our thoughts morph into these amazing newfound actions. Those thoughts also shield us from the arrows of people trying to harm us with their thoughts and words. We no longer have to think like them. The world is not so interesting if it has nothing to do with our Creator and the love he has for us. We have died to the world. We have rendered all that negativity dead and gone, buried with Christ.

How do I control my thoughts?

God gave us a very special gift called "free will." That gift can work in our favor if we use it to purposely partner with the mind and character of Christ. God gives us humans the ability to stand outside of our own thought process and judge it. If you're feeling sad and lonely right now, you can actually:

1. Recognize it.
2. Evaluate it.
3. Choose to change it.

Second Corinthians 10:4–6 outlines it this way: "For the weapons of our warfare are not carnal but mighty in God for pulling down strongholds, casting down arguments and every high thing that exalts itself against the knowledge of God, bringing every thought into captivity to the obedience of Christ, and being ready to punish all disobedience when your obedience is fulfilled."

The definition of "stronghold" is any reasoning that justifies a dysfunction. All the enemies Paul mentions here concerning spiritual warfare are enemies that live in your mind. Being able to recognize and replace a thought that is not in God's mind is the key to healing your body and soul from past trauma. Notice the passage that says "every thought" needs to be taken captive. That's a big responsibility but also an ever-increasing reward to continue to mind-shift your way into your new identity.

How do I hear God?

Jesus taught that there were two prerequisites to hearing his voice:

1. You have to be a sheep. "My sheep hear My voice, and I know them, and they follow Me." (John 10:27)

2. You have to be of the truth. "Pilate therefore said to Him, 'Are You a king then?' Jesus answered, 'You say rightly that I am a king. For this cause I was born, and for this cause I have come into the world, that I should bear witness to the truth. Everyone who is of the truth hears My voice.'" (John 18:37)

The way to hear God is to listen. Don't disqualify yourself, and don't over complicate things. He paid a high price to talk with you. He will always be willing to communicate with you through means and methods that you understand. Sometimes I hear a song. Other times, I have dreams that come true or that help me understand things going on in my life.

To my knowledge, I've never heard the audible voice of God, but I've heard thoughts in my head in my voice. It's important to know who is speaking to you in your thoughts. Satan incited King David to count the men after God told him not to. David listened to the wrong voice. If you aren't sure who is talking, dive into the Bible. If the voice can align with the Word of God, it's God. If not, stay away and ignore it. For instance, if you believe you are worthless and will never amount to anything, look in the Bible. Would Jesus ever say that about his beautiful bride? No. Remember, King David was told directly by God not to count the men. He second-guessed and counted them. He disobeyed. Sometimes we hear God's voice and choose not to listen.

We are asked two questions every day:

1. What did God say?

2. Did God really say...?

Clearly, God is asking the first question. He wants us to hear him and know his love for us, so he asks, "What did I say about...?" He wants us to believe him.

Satan is asking the second question—"Did God really say...?" That's what he did to Eve in the garden. He wants us to question God and God's motives.

Be wise and think about the Father's heart toward you. This will help in making decisions.

CPSIA information can be obtained
at www.ICGtesting.com
Printed in the USA
LVHW080609170720
660706LV00004BA/148